TO KNOW JESUS AS THE CHRIST
Incentives for a Deeper Faith

CHRISTOPH CARDINAL SCHÖNBORN

To Know Jesus as the Christ

Incentives for a Deeper Faith

EDITED BY
HUBERT PHILIPP WEBER

TRANSLATED BY
MICHAEL J. MILLER

IGNATIUS PRESS   SAN FRANCISCO

Original German edition:
Christoph Schönborn, *Jesus als Christus erkennen.*
Impulse zur Vertiefung des Glaubens
Edited by Hubert Philipp Weber
© 2002 by Verlag Herder GmbH, Freiburg im Breisgau
Published by arrangement with Crossroad Publishing

Cover art:
Baptism of Christ, Perugino/Restored Traditions

Cover design by Riz Boncan Marsella

© 2014 by Ignatius Press, San Francisco
All rights reserved
ISBN 978-1-58617-792-8
Library of Congress Control Number 2013917066
Printed in the United States of America ∞

Contents

Preliminary Remark by a Listener

When the Second Vatican Council comes to speak about the duties of bishops, it mentions, first of all, proclaiming the Word of God and, afterward, administering the sacraments and governing.[1] Proclaiming the Word of God is a many-faceted challenge, which by no means is restricted to preaching alone. The archbishop of Vienna, Cardinal Christoph Schönborn, invites believers once a month to strengthen their faith for an hour in Saint Stephen's Cathedral in Vienna, where in a regular series he addresses the central questions of the faith and seeks in today's language to give an answer drawn from the rich treasure of tradition. Each time several hundred people gather to listen to such a catechesis by the cardinal. What had begun as a preparation for the young participants in the 1996 World Youth Day has meanwhile become an hour of faith for Christians of widely varying ages.

Since the often difficult themes demand the complete concentration of the listeners, a request was soon made for a readable text of the catecheses so that the listeners could follow them more easily. For this reason, the spoken texts were transcribed from tape recordings and distributed to those interested. In order to make them accessible to a broader public, these transcriptions were condensed and revised by the

---

[1] Vatican Council II, Dogmatic Constitution on the Church *Lumen gentium* (November 21, 1964), 21.

editor. In many places, the spoken word was deliberately allowed to come through. Anyone who reads them should also participate in the liveliness of the catechesis. Many contemporary references to the life of the Church in Vienna were omitted, because they could be understood only with difficulty by a wider readership. References to the life of the Roman Catholic Church in general were kept, especially allusions to the Holy Year 2000. The local Church is firmly anchored in the Universal Church, and the bishop is the guarantor for this connection.

An essential part of catechesis is the connection between theology and life, between doctrine and practice. The most important source for this is no doubt Sacred Scripture, which offers guidance and light. Besides this, many ecclesiastical texts should be mentioned: the documents of the Second Vatican Council, for instance, or passages from the *Catechism of the Catholic Church* (CCC). Many saints and theologians, too, have their say. Scripture passages are referenced in parentheses. There are also recommendations for further reading at the end of the book. This is mainly a list of shorter works that are comprehensible even for those who have no special theological training.

This book contains in chronological sequence all the catecheses from the academic year 2000–2001. The most important goal of catechesis is to strengthen faith. Moreover, the most important theme is always faith itself: How does it come about? What are its sources? Upon what can it be built anew again and again? Each one-year cycle travels a particular stretch of this catechetical way. This volume traces the contents of our Profession of Faith.

The first catechesis is entitled "God Is One and Triune". The catechetical way begins with God. This, however, is not so much a refined theological doctrine about the Trinity, incorporating all the terminology and controversies, but rather a response to the question: How is it possible in the first place for us to speak about the one God as Father, Son, and Holy Spirit? What does Sacred Scripture say about this? The key is the encounter with Jesus Christ, who addresses God as Father and came to us in order to make us his Father's children.

God is mighty; indeed, we profess that he is *almighty*. The second catechesis investigates this article of faith, showing that God's power and mercy toward those who turn to God confidently are not in contradiction with each other.

The third catechesis connects two questions: God's providence and the big, difficult problem of why God allows evil. The great havoc in the world seems to be incompatible with God's loving care for all creatures. Faith cannot prevent suffering, but it helps us to bear it and to help others bear it.

A Christian understanding of suffering becomes apparent only to someone who knows about the mystery of the Cross and, thus, about our mysterious redemption in Jesus Christ. The fourth catechesis takes as its theme the center of our faith: the fact that salvation for all mankind and the whole world comes from Jesus Christ and only from him. That is a difficult question, particularly in the dialogue with other religions, but no one who believes in Jesus Christ can pass it by.

For the sake of our salvation, Jesus wanted *one* Church. But what does the Church look like today? Many divisions have distorted the Church's face. And yet we believe that in the Catholic Church the true Church of Jesus Christ is realized, as the Second Vatican Council emphasized. But what about the other Churches and ecclesial communities? And by what inner strength are efforts for Church unity sustained? The fifth catechesis deals with the fundamental questions about the Church and her unity, even where this unity is not evident.

Essential to the mystery of Jesus Christ are the miracles and signs that are handed down to us in the Gospels. A lot depends on the status of our faith in Jesus Christ. Where faith is lacking, not even miracles can accomplish anything. If faith is already present, however, then miracles can strengthen it.

The Easter mystery is discussed in the seventh catechesis. To allow one's faith to be strengthened means to go along with the disciples from Emmaus and to let Jesus himself explain by means of the Old Testament why the Messiah had to suffer so much. The Church walks such a path every year in the celebration of the Easter Vigil, when the seven readings from the Old Testament are read.

The eighth catechesis, which was given in May, the month of Mary, deals with experiences of Mary as a helper and the connection between authentic Marian devotion and faith in Jesus Christ, the one Mediator.

The first catechesis starts with God, from whom all good things come, and the last one ends with him, toward whom everything strives. Hope for eternal life is an indispensable part of faith. Yet are we aware that hope for a life with Christ is more than and something quite different from an empty promise?

A shepherd's duty is to lead. And so the archbishop of Vienna leads his listeners and readers here along a catechetical path. In doing so, he also points out stumbling blocks and wrong ways, dangers along the road and places that are difficult to get past. Those who accompany him along this way can experience firsthand a strengthening of their faith and can deepen their knowledge of the faith and become acquainted with new as well as old paths of Christian life.

HUBERT PHILIPP WEBER

I

God Is One and Triune

The Catechetical Way

Catechesis is something different from a theological discourse or a lecture or a sermon. Catechesis is actually a way, and we are invited to set out on such a catechetical way. For catechesis is very closely connected with the mission of Jesus himself. It is actually the direct translation of his mission, which he gave to the apostles at the end of his earthly life in Galilee: "All authority in heaven and on earth has been given to me. Go therefore and make disciples of all nations" (Mt 28:18–19). This, therefore, is the commission given to the Eleven at that time, to their successors, and, through them, to the whole Church: Make disciples of all nations, of all people. The innermost meaning of catechesis is to help people to become disciples of Jesus, or to become so even more fully.

How is this supposed to happen? What does Jesus himself say about it? How does he make people his disciples through his apostles? He says two things: "*baptizing* them in the name of the Father and of the Son and of the Holy Spirit", and secondly: "*teaching* them to observe all that I have commanded you" (Mt 28:19–20). Baptism and teaching. Being plunged into the life of Jesus himself, into the life of the triune God: that is the way in which men become disciples. In this manner they belong to Christ, they receive and share his life. And part of this way is: "*teaching* them to observe all that I have commanded you", in other words, by handing on my teaching. And for this purpose he gave a "guarantee": "and behold, I am with you always, to the close of the age" (Mt 28:20). Catechesis through baptism, through teaching, therefore, occurs in the knowledge that the Lord is with us, always, even today.

Many today are baptized, are already disciples of Jesus. Through baptism they have been plunged into his life. But we are all on the way, in order to become *more fully* disciples, *thoroughly* Christian. When Ignatius of Antioch (d. after 110) was on the way to Rome, where he expected and then in fact suffered martyrdom, he said: "Now I am finally becoming a Christian."[1] He knows that he is still en route. The Catechism says this about the catechetical way: "Quite early on, the name *catechesis* was given to the totality of the Church's efforts to make disciples, to help men believe that Jesus is the Son of God so that believing they might have life in his name, and to educate and instruct them in this life, thus building up the body of Christ" (CCC 4). This passage contains an allusion to the final sentence of [chapter 20 of] the Gospel of John, where John says that all this was written down "that you may believe that Jesus is the Christ, the Son of God, and that believing you may have life in his name" (Jn 20:31).

The first basic catechesis is the Gospel, what the disciples of Jesus wrote down about his life, his public ministry, and about Jesus himself. Through the Gospel he is *the Catechist* who leads us to himself through his Word and his life. This is to say, however, that catechesis has a decisive role in bringing people into contact with Jesus. To know him means to live. To know him means to have eternal life. In his prayer on the night before he suffered, Jesus prayed: "Father, . . .

---

[1] Ignatius of Antioch, *Epistle to the Romans*, chaps. 2–4.

this is eternal life, that they know you the only true God, and Jesus Christ whom you have sent" (Jn 17:1, 3). *To know* Jesus means not only to acknowledge him intellectually but to be united with him, to become one with him, to be one with Jesus, as he is one with the Father. In this farewell prayer, on the night before he suffered, Jesus prays for his disciples: "that they may be one even as we are one, I in them and you in me, that they may become perfectly one [in love and in unity], so that the world may know that you have sent me and have loved them even as you have loved me" (Jn 17:22–23). To know the Father, to know Jesus Christ —we see in the saints, in a man like John XXIII, of whom many still have a living memory, what it means to be a man united with God, someone who not only knows Jesus intellectually but has known him in the biblical sense and is known by him. Such a person is united with him, lives with him.

The Trinity as a Mystery of Faith

We ask the living, triune God in three Persons that we may know him better, love him more, and that we may live more fully in him. Every liturgy begins with the Sign of the Cross: "In the name of the Father and of the Son and of the Holy Spirit." Everywhere God in three Persons stands at the beginning. That is the essence of our faith; the whole Christian faith consists of the Trinity, and we can genuinely say that catechesis has no other goal than to lead people into the communion of the triune God. Of course the mystery of the Trinity is a *mystery of faith.*

There is a well-known legend from the life of Augustine (d. 430): As he was walking along the shore near Hippo, he saw a child playing, who was scooping water out of the sea and pouring it into a hole in the sand. When asked, "What are you doing there?" the child said, "I am pouring the sea into this hole." Augustine told him, "You will never succeed; it is impossible." The child allegedly told him: "I will sooner be able to pour the sea into this hole in the sand than you will be able to fathom the mystery of the Trinity." For twenty years Augustine worked on the book *De Trinitate* (On the Trinity). In those twenty years he struggled, in one approach after another, to formulate the mystery of the Trinity and to find possible ways of expressing it in our wretched language.

The Trinity is the quintessence of the Christian faith. Therefore, the acceptance or the rejection of this mystery is decisive for the whole Christian faith. The pivotal point of our faith in the triune God is, of course, the belief that Jesus is the Son of God. Again and again it is claimed, and we can read in popular literature that is critical of the Church, that belief in the Trinity was a fourth-century invention. Greek philosophy allegedly worked its way into Christianity in this regard and changed the original, simple, biblical faith. Christians supposedly adapted to the times and "invented", so to speak, the dogma of the Trinity. That is decidedly incorrect.

The fundamental question is much older—it is as old as the Christian faith itself. It is the question of whether Jesus is the Messiah, the Son of God. For if Jesus is the Son of God, then he is "God from God, Light from Light, true God from true God, begotten, not made, consubstantial with the Father", as we say in the great Profession of Faith. The decisive question is therefore: Is Jesus really the Son of God?

The philosopher Immanuel Kant (d. 1804) thought that the doctrine of the Trinity contained nothing practical for human reason and was, so to speak, a useless word game of the theologians. But let us try a different approach. If Jesus is not the Son of God, if he is not consubstantial with the Father, then Jesus did not reveal the Father to us, either. Then Jesus cannot reveal God at all. Then he cannot bring us God's life, either, for he can reveal to us only what he knows. But then he did not bring us the forgiveness of sins, either. If Jesus is only a man, a perhaps perfect man, but still only a man, then he cannot be the Redeemer, either. Then we are not redeemed, then we have not been freed from our sins and from death. Everything in our faith depends on the acknowledgment that Jesus is the Son of the living God.

In a catechesis in Rome, the Holy Father [John Paul II] meditated very impressively on the words of the apostle Thomas, who had not been with the others in the Cenacle during the first appearance of Jesus. When Jesus came back eight days after Easter and showed him his wounds, Thomas said to Jesus, "My Lord and my God!" (Jn 20:28). For Jewish ears, that is atrocious, for someone who himself grew up in the Jewish faith tradition, which so decisively and unambiguously says: "Our God is one Lord", "God is one" (cf. Deut 6:4, for example). How can Thomas, the apostle, say to Jesus, who meets him as the Risen One, "My Lord and my God"?

To Proclaim Jesus as the Christ

If Jesus is not the Son of God, naturally there is no Trinity; then everything is in fact useless wordplay. We have only one access to the mystery of the Trinity: only Jesus himself. Jesus is the one who reveals to us that God is our Father, that he is the Son, and to that end he sent us the Holy Spirit. He revealed God as the Father by the fact that he himself is the

Son and that we are all called to be children of this Father, just as he is Son of the Father. But we become children of God by grace. We remain children of men and yet become children of God, sons and daughters of the Father. Pope John Paul II says in his great letter on catechesis: "Catechesis aims at putting 'people . . . in communion . . . with Jesus Christ: only he can lead us to the love of the Father in the Spirit and make us share in the life of the Holy Trinity.'"[2]

Catechesis is, therefore, first and foremost about Jesus Christ and about everything else only with regard to him. Christ is the Teacher, and we are teachers only insofar as we hand on Christ's Word and enable Christ, so to speak, to teach through the mouth of the catechist. The pope says in this document about catechesis: "Every catechist should be able to apply to himself the mysterious words of Jesus: 'My teaching is not mine, but his who sent me.'"[3] "The word which you hear is not mine but the Father's who sent me" (Jn 14:24). And so, the pope says, every catechist should be able to say about himself: My teaching is not my teaching but the teaching of him who sent me. To teach Christ, to make Christ known, works only if we ourselves know him. Hence, the first task of catechesis is to become better acquainted ourselves with Jesus so as to be able to witness to him. The catechist must be ready to suffer "the loss of all things", as Paul says, "in order . . . [to] gain Christ and be found in him, . . . [to] know him and the power of his resurrection, and [to] share his sufferings" (Phil 3:8–10).

From this knowledge comes the desire to evangelize, to invite and encourage others to say Yes in faith to Jesus Christ. "To proclaim the Gospel today" is a concern that Clement

---

[2] John Paul II, Apostolic Exhortation *Catechesi Tradendae* (October 16, 1979), 5 (CCC 426).

[3] Ibid., 6 (CCC 427), cf. Jn 7:16.

Maria Hofbauer, the patron saint of the city of Vienna, brings to our attention, as it were. This can only mean bringing people into communion with Christ, making this communion concrete for them, and, as it were, enticing them to it.

The Life and Work of Jesus

How did the disciples of Jesus, how did the people who met Jesus, know that he is the Son of God? How did this faith come about? After all, it is not an invention of theologians but, rather, the acknowledgment of people who have come to know Jesus and to love him. First we are confronted with the great riddle, the fact that for thirty years Jesus remained hidden with his mystery, with his identity. Only in Mary's heart was the promise alive, along with the knowledge that she bore within herself, in faith, of who this child was that grew up in Nazareth, matured into a young man, and took up the carpenter's trade, as Joseph had done. Mary treasured in her heart for thirty years what she believed on the strength of the angel's message. What must that have been like, quietly carrying in her heart something that was not expressed, something that was so hidden: "He will be great, and will be called the Son of the Most High" (Lk 1:32)? We know nothing about this time; the veil is lifted only once, when the twelve-year-old Jesus was sought by his parents for three days in Jerusalem. Then when they found him in the temple, we read this puzzling remark that describes in advance all the rest of his life. Mary says to him: "Son, why have you treated us so? . . . Your father and I have been looking for you anxiously." And he answers: "Did you not know that I must be in my Father's house?" (Lk 2:48–49). We read that they did not understand what he was saying but that Mary

kept it in her heart (Lk 2:50–51). Jesus speaks about "*my*
Father". The center of his life is there, his heart is there,
that is the place to which he is drawn and from which he
comes.

We do not know how that looked in his everyday life,
but one saying of the twelve-year-old to his parents will accompany him throughout the rest of his life: ". . . that I
must be in my Father's house". This *necessity* characterizes
his entire life down to the disciples in Emmaus, to whom he
would say: "*Was it not necessary* that the Christ should suffer
these things and enter into his glory?" (Lk 24:26). Jesus has
something that he must do in his life, on his way. But this
is not a compulsion, rather, it is what the Father wills for
him and wants of him. Later he will say: "My food is to
do the will of [my Father]" (Jn 4:34). He lives on what the
Father wills; this is vitally necessary for him, his life support. When we look at Jesus' life, then we see that he is not
slavish, not confined. He does not feel pressured by this will
of the Father, by this necessity in his life, but, rather, feels
quite free. He says Yes to it: that is the center of his life.

Jesus stands under this necessity when he then at age
thirty goes public, first to the Jordan to allow himself to
be baptized, then into the desert, and then back to Galilee,
to Capernaum, where he takes up residence and where his
public life, his ministry, begins. Here the Gospels begin to
take away the veil over his life and to give an insight into
what he says and does. When he begins to teach there, he
speaks above all about God as the Father. If we take the Sermon on the Mount, the Father is always the central point
in it. It is important, he says, not to be seen by men but,
rather, "by your Father who is in heaven" (cf. Mt 6:1–4).
He speaks about "your father" with an intimacy and a ten-
derness that are possible only because he knows the Father.

He speaks also in parables about the Father. The most famous is probably the parable of the merciful father and the prodigal son (Lk 15:11–32). But when we look closer, Jesus always speaks about himself, also, for when he speaks about the Father, he speaks about the one whom he is privileged to call Father. He can speak about him as none of the learned scribes can. The listeners say: Never before have we heard a man speak this way; none of the scribes ever spoke like this.

Jesus does not speak theoretically, based on what he has learned after the manner of the scribes, who know Scripture well and interpret it. Jesus speaks based on what he has immediately seen and heard of the Father. He knows who the Father is; he knows him. That is why he can speak about God in a way in which only someone who is himself God can speak—someone who personally knows how God feels, what moves God's heart. That is why Jesus can then also bring himself into play in a way that no rabbi would ever have dared to do. That provokes great resistance, for example when he says already in the Sermon on the Mount: "You have heard that it was said to the men of old, 'You shall not kill. . . .' But I say to you that . . . whoever says, 'You fool!' shall be liable to the hell of fire" (Mt 5:21–22). "But *I* say to you. . . ." No rabbi would have dared to speak in that way. Jesus speaks with an inimitable authority, which goes so far as this unthinkable saying: "Heaven and earth will pass away, but my words will not pass away" (Mt 24:35). Can that ever have been said by a man—a man who is only a human being? If that were the statement of a man who was only a human being, then one would have to tell him that he was totally arrogant, presumptuous, indeed, insane. Jesus not only speaks this way but also acts this way, as is befitting no man. At his mere word, the storm subsides and the sea is calmed (Mt 14:22–33). The apostles fall down before him and say, "You are the Son of God" (Mt 14:33).

Jesus speaks not only about the Father but also about himself. And when he speaks about himself, then it is not as some accuse him: "You make yourself God" (cf. Jn 19:7). Rather, he says what he sees and hears of the Father, and he can say: "The Father . . . has himself borne witness to me" (cf. Jn 5:37). The figure of Jesus provokes astonishment, fear, but also joy. "Who is this?" the people ask again and again (for example, Lk 5:21; 7:49). And finally it comes down to the decisive question that Jesus asks the disciples at Caesarea Philippi: "But who do you say that I am?" Peter answers: "You are the Christ, the Son of the living God" (Mt 16:15–16).

But it cannot be overlooked that this intimacy with the Father gave offense. Very early on, people said, "He blasphemes against God", "no man can say that", for example when he healed the crippled man who had been let down at his feet through the roof and said to him: "Child, your sins are forgiven" (Mk 2:5–7). Then some of those present grumbled and said: "Who can forgive sins but God alone?" (Mk 2:7). As a result, there are entirely contradictory judgments about Jesus. For some he is out of his mind, he is even possessed by a demon, while for others he is the Messiah, the Son of God. And what does Jesus himself say about it? In the Gospel of Luke, we read that Jesus rejoiced in the Holy Spirit. It breaks out of his heart, as it were; what he bears in his heart is forced into the open: his intimacy with the Father. Jesus says: "I thank you, Father, Lord of heaven and earth, that you have hidden these things from the wise and understanding and revealed them to infants; yes, Father, for such was your gracious will" (Lk 10:21). And then he adds: "All things have been delivered to me by my Father; and no one knows who the Son is except the Father, or who the Father is except the Son and any one to whom the Son chooses to reveal him" (Lk 10:22). No one knows the Son except the Father.

To know Jesus as the Christ is therefore not something we can simply learn through a lot of studying, through precise historical research. Really to know Jesus is a gift from God. After Peter said, "You are the Christ, the Son of the living God", Jesus replied: "Blessed are you, Simon Bar-Jona! For flesh and blood has not revealed this to you" (Mt 16:16–17). This means, you did not arrive at this by yourself; it does not come from your own cleverness; rather, "my Father who is in heaven" revealed it. It was the same with the apostle Paul. When he thinks back on how he came to know Jesus, when Jesus suddenly revealed himself to him and he recognized who this Jesus of Nazareth really was, he says later in retrospect about this conversion: "But when he who had set me apart before I was born, and had called me through his grace, was pleased to reveal his Son to me, . . . I did not confer with flesh and blood" (Gal 1:15–16). God revealed his Son to him. And it is no different in the lives of converts, people who come to know Jesus, to whom faith in Jesus is given, to whom Jesus shows himself as the Son of God. My confrere François Dreyfus (d. 1999), a Dominican of Jewish descent, described impressively the significance of this turning point, when this Jesus of Nazareth suddenly shines forth as the Messiah, the Son of God. It is a grace-filled event that no human intellect can bring about. God grants it; he reveals who Jesus is.

Jesus was acknowledged as the Son of God, but how did that
lead to the dogma of the Trinity? Is it not a late develop-
ment that originally was actually much simpler? Is the dogma
of the Trinity not much too complicated? Many preachers
fear Trinity Sunday: What will I preach about? And yet at
the conclusion of the Second Letter to the Corinthians, the
apostle Paul already extends a greeting to the community in
Corinth—we know it from the liturgy: "The grace of the
Lord Jesus Christ and the love of God and the fellowship of
the Holy Spirit be with you all" (2 Cor 13:14). Did Paul
know what he was saying? Did Paul believe in the Most
Holy Trinity? There is a sentence in the First Letter to the
Corinthians that sounds very pensive. What was this Jew,
who believed in the uniqueness of God, thinking when he
wrote to the Corinthians: There are no gods (1 Cor 8:4;
cf. Gal 4:8)? They were at home in a polytheistic world
in which there were many gods. Paul told them that there
were no gods; rather, "there is one God, the Father, from
whom are all things and for whom we exist." Then Paul
goes on to say, much to our surprise: "And one Lord, Jesus
Christ, through whom are all things and through whom we
exist" (1 Cor 8:6). There is only one God, and one is Lord,
Jesus Christ. There are not many gods; we believe in the
one God, and yet Paul says: One God, the Father, and one
Lord, Jesus Christ. "Lord" is a divine name. There are not
two "Gods"; there is one God, and yet we profess the one
Father and the one Lord Jesus Christ.

How did this become a dogma? The apparent contradiction in this sentence of Saint Paul and in many similar sentences had to be cleared up sooner or later. And often the false teachers, the heretics, are the ones who make

such a clarification necessary. In the early fourth century, a priest from Alexandria, Arius (d. around 336), wanted to straighten out, so to speak, this verbal confusion. He said: Let's be clear, there is *only one* God. And everything else that is said about Jesus Christ must be understood in such a way that it does not contradict the one God. Therefore, Jesus Christ is a creature—admittedly, the highest of all creatures —and yet just a creature and not God. On God's side stands God alone, God the Father, and on the creatures' side stands Jesus Christ, in the first place, and then all other creatures. This solution seemed plausible to many, and it won a great number of adherents. Arianism kept the Church holding her breath—or out of breath—for at least three hundred years. A decision was necessary. The first ecumenical council, which was held in 325 in Nicaea, made its decision along different lines from that of Arius: No, Jesus Christ is the *one Lord*, he is "God from God, Light from Light, true God from true God, begotten, not made". He is not a creature but, rather, is the only begotten, eternal Son of the Father. He is "consubstantial with the Father". He is essentially equal to the Father.

For this doctrine, for this faith, many were martyred or went into exile; Saint Athanasius (d. 373) was driven from his episcopal see five times and for a time was almost the only one in the Church who firmly believed that Jesus is true God and true man. I think that today we are in a situation that is not entirely dissimilar. This clear profession that Jesus the Christ is the Son of the living God is called for once again. Many people would like to tone it down; many think that it is too much to expect a reasonable person to accept such a thing. It was not the dogmatic stubbornness of the ancient Church that made her adhere to the article of faith that Jesus is true God, God from God, Light from

Light; rather, it was the experience, the certainty in faith, that the mystery of the Trinity is the great mystery of our faith, that God is an infinite communion of love and self-giving, that God is not the lonely, distant one but, rather, is infinitely alive and is in himself a communion of Father, Son, and Holy Spirit.

Faith Experiences of the Triune God

I am sure that there are many people who in their simple, straightforward faith firmly and certainly believe that God is Three and One, even if they cannot explain it (no one can explain it). During the year in which I lived in Rome, my residence was not far from La Storta on the Via Cassia. Again and again I got onto a bus or a train in La Storta and had the opportunity to visit a little chapel there alongside the road on the Via Cassia—an indescribable little chapel that has great importance in the history of the Church. Ignatius of Loyola (d. 1556) was making his way to Rome, traveling on the Via Cassia, which leads to Rome from the north, with some of his companions. When they were a few kilometers from Rome, they stopped at this little chapel. There Ignatius had an experience, a vision, a personal encounter that left a mark on the rest of his life and, in fact, decisively influenced his foundation. He saw in an interior image, in a vision, how God the Father was speaking to Jesus, his Son, who was carrying the Cross, and how he commended Ignatius and his companions to his Son: "Take them into your society, into your company!" And Jesus turned with a loving glance toward Ignatius and said to him: "I will be gracious to you in Rome (*Romae propitius vobis ero*)." That is how tradition puts it: I will be favorable to you in Rome, or: I will be with you. Ignatius himself mentioned this experience again and again; his closest confidants handed it on; and it is said that this is where the name of the Society of Jesus comes from. The Father asked his Son in a way: Take Ignatius into your company, into your society. If that is so, then the name "Society of Jesus" is not arrogant but, rather, a wonderful expression for what Jesus wants to give to us all, what the Father wants to give to us all: that we become companions of Jesus. Jesus appears to Ignatius as someone carrying the Cross and, thus, with the whole burden of what he took upon himself for us, but also with the full expression of his love, with which he turns to Ignatius, accepts the will of the Father, and associates Ignatius and his companions to himself. I think that this vision in La Storta near Rome is something like an archetype of what we believe about the triune God. We come to the Father only through the Son, drawn, guided, supported by the Holy Spirit. And the image that this vision places before our eyes can accompany us. We are allowed to be companions of Jesus, who out of love carries the Cross for us, for the whole world; we have the privilege of being associates of Jesus, to whom the Father has assigned and entrusted this mission so that we might have life. We could mention the experiences of many other saints with the Most Holy Trinity.

In Sunday Vespers the Church prays a hymn that begins with the words: *O lux beata trinitas*, O Light, O Blessed Trinity. I would like to invite you, when making the Sign of the Cross and on other occasions, to practice personally this loving, confident entrusting of self to the Trinity, to turn lovingly to the Trinity, and to make this your path.

II

God, All-Powerful and Powerless?

The LORD is my shepherd, I shall not want;
 he makes me lie down in green pastures.
He leads me beside still waters;
 he restores my soul.
He leads me in the paths of righteousness
 for his name's sake.

Even though I walk through the valley of the shadow
  of death,
 I fear no evil;
for you are with me;
 your rod and your staff,
 they comfort me.

You prepare a table before me
 in the presence of my enemies;
you anoint my head with oil,
 my cup overflows.
Surely goodness and mercy shall follow me
 all the days of my life;
and I shall dwell in the house of the LORD
 for ever. (Psalm 23)

This psalm is a prayer full of trust. What can happen to me?
The Lord is my shepherd! Why should I be afraid in the
dark ravines of my life, along my path? For you are with
me, and your rod and your staff give me confidence! I do

not need to fear my powerful foes, who threaten me from
within or from without. You anoint my head with oil, which
means that you give me strength; you yourself are *mighty*,
all-powerful. Nothing is impossible for you (Jer 32:17; Lk
1:37). And since you are all-good, your almighty power is
kind to us: "The LORD is my shepherd, I shall not want."

God the Almighty

What does it mean when we profess in the Profession of
Faith: "I believe in God, the Father *almighty*"? In placing
this psalm at the beginning, I have already begun to interpret
this article of faith from the Creed. This trust-filled psalm,
which professes that God is my shepherd, professes the same
thing as the first article of our Profession of Faith. This catechesis is supposed to be a further step along our path of
faith and to strengthen us in faith, and that means, first of all,
in the confidence that the Lord is my shepherd, that I have
nothing to fear whenever and wherever he protects me, that
everything is in his hand, and that it is a loving hand that
cares for me. This catechesis, then, is supposed to help us
along in faith. To believe, after all, means decisively to hold
fast to the faith, even contrary to all outward appearances;
to affirm in our understanding and with our will and with
our whole heart that God is the almighty Father, even when
many things appear externally to be quite different and this
faith must therefore stand the test, even when it has to fight.

To believe in the almighty God is an act of trust. To speak
about the almighty God is, in contrast to much that is perhaps associated today with the notion of power and might,
first of all an expression of trust and of hope. God is the
almighty Father; that is an act of hope. When we profess

this, then it is not just information that we communicate to one another but, first of all, an expression of our hope and of our faith. In this way the psalms pray, full of confident hope. Even in affliction, even in need, in danger, the prayerful profession of God's almighty power is a source of hope. So we read, for instance, in Psalm 135: "For I know that the LORD is great, and that our Lord is above all gods. Whatever the LORD pleases he does, in heaven and on earth, in the seas and all deeps" (5–6). This insight, "Yes, he accomplishes everything he wills, he can do anything he pleases", is a prayer of hope. Let us try to draw closer to this hope, to this trust.

There is a poem by the great Saint Teresa of Avila. It is well known and often quoted, a sort of exhortation to trust that gives expression to God's almighty power in an especially beautiful way. This poem says in another way what Psalm 23 expresses: hope and trust that come from faith and that, of course, are also connected with great demands. It begins, in Spanish, with the words, "Nada te turbe. . . ."

> Let nothing trouble you / Let nothing frighten you
> Everything passes / God never changes
> Patience / Obtains all
> Whoever has God / Wants for nothing
> God alone is enough. (CCC 227)

Power, Might, and Responsibility

What we profess: "I believe in God, the Father almighty", we should also try to understand better. Faith desires to understand so as to be able to love better, also. Let us try, therefore, to understand a little better this statement about God's almighty power.

First of all, we should do away with a misunderstanding, a difficulty that strongly affects our understanding today. The word "power" sounds negative, so that many people are, instead, tempted to suppress the word in the liturgy and not to address God in prayer as the all-powerful one, because that sounds overwhelming and domineering and seems not to express kindness and love. Nowadays the word "power" often implies the idea of arbitrariness, as it is expressed particularly in dictators' lust for power, but as it also resonates somewhat indistinctly wherever people speak about power—even in church. Should we, then, speak about God's almighty power at all?

Now it is important, first of all, to remember that the word "power" does not express something negative. In the dictionary, we read that "power" is "the totality of strengths and means that are available to someone or to one thing as opposed to others". That is in principle something positive. To have power means, first of all, to be able to work capably. If I have the power of ambulation, then that is something positive. When a child begins to walk, when it becomes capable of ambulation, then that is a magnificent experience. Gradually this ability to function is manifested and strengthened.

Power means, in the first instance, *bodily strength*, a physical operational capability. We know how important this is from all our everyday tasks. It is beneficial when we can work and difficult when we are hindered in our work, when the body no longer has the power to be active. Then there can be *intellectual capabilities*, and these too are a power, to be able to make, operate, or do something, to bring something about. Among these are *decision-making abilities*. Our whole life is characterized by such decision-making abilities and decisions, which we have to follow and which are by no means always exclusively negative. Jesus gives a beautiful example of this in the Gospel when he marvels at the Roman centurion who asks him to heal his servant and who tells Jesus, "For I am a man under authority, with soldiers under me; and I say to one, 'Go,' and he goes, and to another, 'Come,' and he comes" (Mt 8:9; Lk 7:8)—the power to command. And he expresses his trust in Jesus, his faith that Jesus, too, can speak such a word, a powerful word: "Only say the word, and my servant will be healed" (Mt 8:8; Lk 7:7). A very beautiful example of understanding what God's power means, based on a human experience of power.

Power is, therefore, in itself a positive, indeed, a vitally necessary reality. It begins with the fact that I have power *over myself*, over my abilities, my actions, my thoughts, my imagination, over what I do or omit, as it seems right and important to me, over what I have taken upon myself as a task or what is assigned or entrusted to me. All this means having power over oneself. Saint James mentions a very telling example: power over one's tongue (Jas 3:1–12). How powerful is the person who controls his tongue, and how much abuse of power there is through this little organ, the tongue, which can cause so much mischief.

One much debated topic is joint custody of children after the divorce of their parents—an example in which we see how difficult it is to harmonize one's own power, one's own ability to control and decide, with that of others. How painful *power struggles* are, beginning in the family and extending into all areas of society, politics, business, and even the Church. They are part of our life as soon as there is a lack of mutual consideration and when cooperation becomes weaker than competition. That is why it is so indispensable to control power, in ourselves, in the way in which we deal with our power, but also mutually. Power must be limited, because we are always in danger of *misusing* it. This occurs through all sorts of measures to control and *balance powers.* How horrible it is for a country when that no longer functions. In Ecuador, I learned that in one city of 40,000 inhabitants, the population drove out the police, because they were so corrupt that they committed more crimes than they prevented. When the balance of powers no longer functions, it is a tragedy for the people. A balance of powers occurs, however, not just through the external process of control, but first and foremost through *responsibility* in one's own dealings with power, through being aware that any sort of power that I may have is not simply and arbitrarily at my disposal but, rather, is something for which I am responsible. What do I do with my power? Whether that has to do with my skills in my profession or whether it is authority over other people: What do I do with my power?

Every power implies a *responsibility* to handle it in the manner appropriate to the power itself that is entrusted to me. Bodily power does not exist in order to destroy, even though it makes a person capable of that, but, rather, in order to do good, to help, to work. Intellectual powers exist in order to promote the common good, and not so as to hatch nefarious plots and then carry them out. We see from this that power is in principle something good, which, however, must be used sensibly in a manner that is inherent in the power itself. Jesus expressed this in the parable of the talents (Mt 25:14–30). Something has been entrusted to you. What are you doing with the power that is entrusted to you? It is something magnificent when people act responsibly and rightly with the talent that is entrusted to them, with the power that is placed in their hands. What a blessing! But what a curse it is, even in small matters, when we misuse power.

We are all acquainted with the experience of *powerlessness*, the physical weakness that paralyzes us, that can become a burden to us, indeed, a torment. We know powerlessness, how very limited our own power, our capability is. How painfully parents experience this with regard to their children, to whom they can be an example but whose freedom they cannot determine, whom they must respect even when they follow different paths from those they would have wished. Yes, how vividly we become aware of our own powerlessness when we have to admit that our willpower is not enough to resist the force of habit. One simply cannot get past it with the will. This does not need to be a dramatic situation at all, like, for instance, alcoholism. It already begins in miniature with the ingrained habits against which we often feel powerless. So every human being must admit his own limitations, if only to protect ourselves from the insanity of believing that we are all-powerful, that we can do anything, that everything is possible for us. How quickly the delusion that one can control and do everything leads to a fall into powerlessness. Trees grow tall but stop short of heaven. This is true not only for great dictators, who have all fallen nevertheless; it is true also for our own false dreams and notions that are not built on God.

"With God Nothing Is Impossible"

What, then, does "God's almighty power" mean? The angel says to Mary: "With God nothing will be impossible" (Lk 1:37). Can God do all things? Is anything and everything possible for him, unlike us? In the Book of Wisdom, it says someplace: "God can do all things." "It is always in your power to show great strength" (Wis 11:21). Everything is under your control. At the beginning of this talk, we prayed the psalm: "The LORD is my shepherd, I shall not want" (Ps 23:1). Once again: the profession of God's almighty power is, in the first place, a profession of trust and faith that God is able to do all things. In this faith-filled confidence, we now go on to ask: What is God's power like?

There are many "attributes" of God. We say that God is all-present, all-knowing, all-good, all-merciful. But, oddly enough, in the Creed only his almighty power is mentioned, none of the other qualities that are attributed to God. Why is his almighty power emphasized in particular? First of all, probably because immediately afterward comes the profession that God is the *Creator of heaven and earth*. The Creed says that everything that exists comes from God, was brought about by his power. Nothing comes from itself; nothing made itself. Even though science tries to develop a theory that matter organized itself, we believe and know in faith that it cannot be that the world made itself. God created everything out of nothing. Everything is in his hands. But that also means that his creative power extends to everything, because everything owes its existence to him. Nothing is, so to speak, out of his hands. In faith, we are quite certain of this. Even if we cannot prove it scientifically, we are nevertheless convinced of it, and there is much evidence that this faith conviction is important and sensible. I know that the whole universe, life, my soul, my mind, everything is created by God; nothing made itself. I know that not only what I have and am, but also all that I can do, all activity in nature, all activity in the cosmos, all activity in spiritual creatures, in human beings, is given by God. I gave myself neither my life nor my existence nor my thinking, willing, or feeling. It was all given to me as a gift by my almighty Creator. I know this in faith, even though it is hidden and concealed.

When we recite this article from the Creed, we believe it

irrespective of outward appearances. It seems that the world in which we live, of which I am a part and which strongly influences me, runs as though it came entirely from itself, as if it were self-sufficient, as though God did not exist. Science and commerce function, at least viewed externally, as though there were no God and as though we had no need of God. Indeed, they are so powerful, so imposing, so fascinating, that sometimes we get the impression that they are the "gods of our age". With the end of Communism, the free market system triumphed throughout the world. Its power is unlimited; everything has to be subordinated to this power. Factual constraints, economic forces, everything has to be subordinated to the "god of the market". If we reflect on the immense influence of the media world, from earliest childhood until advanced old age, and what sort of ideas and understanding of life this media world brings with it, we have the impression that there is no room in this world for an all-powerful God. It is so powerful in and of itself, it has such power with its images, with the ideas that it conveys, that it is a god unto itself.

In the nineteenth century, Friedrich Nietzsche (d. 1900), the philosopher, spoke about the death of God, which at that time was still something quite dramatic and shocking. Sometimes it almost seems that this statement has meanwhile crept into and increasingly infiltrated our world and has become something self-evident. The world lives as though God did not exist. With the deciphering of the genetic code, many have already declared man to be the new god, who will take everything into his hand and in the future will determine everything by himself.

Somehow this talk about almighty God is particularly offensive today. It seems to be so far away from the reality in which we live, from the practical atheism of our time, which is quite different from the militant atheism of

Communism, which still fought openly and directly against church and religion. Today's creeping atheism is much more thoroughgoing and is noticed much less. Sometimes God seems to be quite powerless against it. Where can almighty God be found here? All other powers seem more powerful than the all-powerful: the market, the media, public opinion, and this-worldly life in general, "the last chance" that must be exploited fully, because afterward comes nothing anyway. What good, then, is it to profess belief in almighty God? We must ask ourselves the question: How far has this creeping atheism taken up residence in our hearts as well, so that we hear the statement by Saint Teresa of Avila, "Dios solo basta", "God alone suffices", almost as though it were in a foreign language?

Often we encounter an additional question: "If you say that he is all-powerful, then why in his omnipotence does he not prevent so much misery in the world?" If God is really all-powerful, why can he not prevent evil? Why was it possible for this endless flood of evil and suffering in the twentieth century to exist? Let us try to approach the concept of almighty power once again. Does this mean that God can do everything whatsoever that is possible, including things that are totally senseless and arbitrary? Could he, for example, command that good is evil and evil is good? Can he do something wicked or nonsensical? Can he square the circle or make wood out of iron, in other words, do things that are senseless or contradictory?

Christ—"The Power of God and the Wisdom of God"

In conclusion, I would like to attempt an answer to the pressing question of our time, whether God has become totally absent. Do we see God as the powerless one and not as the Almighty? What does it actually mean to believe that *God became man*? We believe that this really happened. Jesus is the eternal Son of God, who really became man of Mary. With that we profess, after all, that God is mighty. Indeed, the greatest sign of his power is that he completely and voluntarily humbled himself and became a man, a child —humbled himself even unto the Cross and rose again from the dead. We believe with Saint Paul that Christ, the Cruci-fied One, is "the power of God and the wisdom of God". "The foolishness of God is wiser than men, and the weak-ness of God is stronger than men" (1 Cor 1:24–25). If we inquire into the almighty power of God, then we must look squarely at what is the greatest proof of his omnipotence: God is so powerful that he can become as small as a child. God's power is best manifested in Christ's self-emptying. It is difficult for us to accept this revelation of his almighty power. His disciples had trouble with it to the end. Right before the Ascension, they asked him: Will you now finally establish the Kingdom? Will you finally show your power now (cf. Acts 1:6)? He did not show him the power they expected; rather, he showed the power of his love, which is expressed in the Cross and Resurrection.

Three thoughts, three key passages, should show how we can live out our faith in God's almighty power in a time when so many other powers seem to be much more power-ful than the all-powerful God.

1. When his disciples were once quarreling about who among them was the greatest—power struggles that existed then in the Church and still exist to this day—Jesus said to them, "You know that rulers oppress their peoples and the powerful misuse their power over others. It shall not be so among you, but whoever among you wants to be great must become the servant of all" (cf. Mt 20:25–26 and

parallel passages). If we want to understand God's almighty power, then we must *follow Jesus*, even to the place where he most clearly showed his power, in his service. "I . . . , your . . . Teacher, have washed your feet" (Jn 13:14). You correctly call me Teacher, "for so I am" (Jn 13:13). We recognize the mysterious reality of God's almighty power to the extent that we follow Jesus along the way on which he showed the Father's almighty power, through his self-giving service unto the sacrifice of his life.

2. In one Opening Prayer at Mass, we read: "God, you show your almighty power above all *in your mercy and forgiveness.*"[1] With that the Church means to tell us: God's almighty power is manifested wherever he does what only divine freedom can do. We have misused our freedom, our power, and have acted against God's will, against one another, and against ourselves. God in his sovereign freedom can remedy that. He can have mercy on us and forgive us our sins. Therein his almighty power is displayed.

3. After the war, Father Petrus Pavlicek, O.F.M., on the basis of an interior locution, believed that Mary is so powerful in her intercession that she could bring about even the liberation of Austria. That is why he trusted in her intercession and persuaded hundreds of thousands of people to entrust themselves to Mary and to implore her intercession for their country, for all their cares and concerns. In Mary we see the *power of faith*. At Cana, Mary said: "Do whatever he tells you" (Jn 2:5). In this confidence she was able, so to speak, to open the floodgates of God's almighty power. We may correctly assume that it was her intercession that ultimately gave Austria its freedom. The most powerful are the humblest. They have, so to speak, "the greatest influ-

---

[1] Twenty-sixth Sunday in Ordinary Time; CCC 277.

ence on God's heart". That is why Mary is for us also an image—an icon, one might almost say—in which we see what it means to trust in God's almighty power.

To speak about almighty God is, first and foremost, to speak about hope. If God is all-powerful, then nothing can separate us any more from the love of God.

III

What Does Divine Providence Mean?
God's Goodness and the Problem of Evil

Two topics come together in this catechesis. I had prepared a catechesis for November 12, 2000; the announced topic was "Divine Providence". It was very moving for me to prepare this catechesis on that particular day, because how is someone supposed to speak about God's providence in view of the catastrophe in Kaprun? The second part, "God's Goodness and the Problem of Evil", once again treats the same topic, in terms of the great question: How does God's kindly hand work also in the misfortune or even in the evil that we encounter? If God is good, then how can evil exist? If God loves us, then why does he allow us to suffer? Does evil have a place in his providence? And, if so, what place? Is it God's punishment when disaster befalls us? Or, if everything really is in his hands, is it God's plan that misfortunes and catastrophes happen?

In the morning hours of November 11, 2000, 155 people died in a fire in the tunnel of the Gletscherbahn 2 funicular railway in Kaprun during a trip to the Kitzsteinhorn. In the evening of the following Sunday, November 12, 2000, the archbishop of Vienna celebrated the Eucharist in Saint Stephen's Cathedral in memory of the victims. The cathedral was filled with an immense number of the faithful, who were visibly shocked, and they remained in the cathedral after the liturgy for silent prayer. The catechesis about divine providence had been planned and prepared for that evening. Together with the following one about God's goodness and the problem of evil, it still affected many people personally a month later.—EDITOR

Everything in God's Hands

First, I would like to quote four passages from Sacred Scripture, so that we can become attuned to this topic. For if there is an answer to the question, we must seek it in the Word of God, in what God has said to us concerning this puzzling question, perhaps the most puzzling of all. The first Scripture passage is from the prophet Isaiah. God tells us through the prophet: "I am the LORD, and there is no other, besides me there is no God. . . . I form light and create darkness, I make well-being and create woe, I am the LORD, who do all these things" (Is 45:5–7). In an absolute way here, everything—light and darkness, well-being and woe—is placed in God's hands.

A second passage also comes from the Old Testament: Hannah, the mother of Samuel, is barren and pours out her sorrow in tears in the house of God in the presence of Eli, the priest. One year later, she comes back with a child, with her son, Samuel, in her arms. She sings a song of praise, a hymn of thanksgiving to the Lord, in which we read: "The LORD kills and brings to life; he brings down to Sheol and raises up. The LORD makes poor and makes rich; he brings low, he also exalts" (1 Sam 2:6–7). We hear echoes of the Magnificat, Mary's hymn of praise, in which she alludes to Hannah's song of praise when she sings that God "has put down the mighty from their thrones, and exalted those of low degree" (Lk 1:52). Sacred Scripture, therefore, attributes everything to God. Everything comes from his hand: life and death, happiness and suffering. But in Sacred Scripture, this is not fatalism and most certainly not belief in some blind destiny. Both the prophet Isaiah and Hannah, the mother of Samuel, expressed in these words a profound trust, trust in God: All is in his hands.

The third passage to testify to this is from the Book of Job. Job is a pagan, who is held up to Israel as a just man. He is struck by unimaginable calamity: all of his wealth, his whole family, everything is taken from him. After all this happens, he says: "Naked I came from my mother's womb, and naked shall I return; the LORD gave, and the LORD has taken away; blessed be the name of the LORD" (Job 1:21). When in a second wave even his physical health is taken away and he sits there covered with sores and his wife says to him, "Curse God!" he replies: "Shall we receive good at the hand of God, and shall we not receive evil?" And a comment is added: "In all this Job did not sin with his lips" (Job 2:9–10). We see here the model of a man who accepts everything from God's hand: Thy will be done!

The fourth passage, from the New Testament, testifies to *Jesus' own attitude*. In Gethsemane, in agony before his death, Jesus expressed his final self-abandonment to the will of his Father: "Abba, Father, all things are possible to you; remove this chalice from me; yet not what I will, but what you will" (Mk 14:36). And the Father's will was that Jesus should not be saved from that hour but, instead, that he should drink the "bitter chalice" of his suffering to the dregs, until his loud cry, "Eli, Eli, lama sabachthani?"—"My God, my God, why have you forsaken me?" (Mt 27:46; cf. Ps 22:1).

The message of the Bible is therefore: Resign yourself to the will of God. God's will, even if it is obscure and incomprehensible, is good for us. "Thy will be done", we pray in the Our Father. This trust, this total entrusting of self to the will of the Father, is then also the last word that Jesus speaks on the Cross: "Father, into your hands I commit my spirit" (Lk 23:46).

Chance—Fate—a Plan?

This, then, is what faith says. It is also the experience of so many people who have lived their lives based on this faith. The pastor of Kaprun told me how significant it was for him to experience the faith witness of people who endured these difficult hours in faith. Yet a big riddle remains. I come back once again to November 11, Saint Martin's day. Certainly there is already some distance from those events now, and yet major questions remain, which we cannot avoid: Did God allow that? Does such a catastrophe have a place in God's plans?

Did God allow that, or was it simply chance? What must it be like for those who by chance came too late and could not ride in that railcar, the woman who had forgotten her gloves and went back to get them and so was not on the train, those who were unhappy that they could not go skiing that day and had to stay home? What about those who managed at the last minute to get onto that railcar so as to be on the slopes sooner and thus rode to their deaths? Is there a plan behind all that, or is it destiny, or is it chance? And if it is not simply destiny or chance, if it was not, so to speak, written in the stars and did not blindly overtake the victims, how can we see God's loving hand behind it? But, conversely, if there is no divine providence, then do our lives not simply run down according to the laws of blind caprice?

First, two sober preliminary comments. For those who are affected, the question is posed not in the abstract but *concretely and personally*: A human being who is dear to them, or even more than one, is suddenly snatched from life by death. Their question is just as personal as their grief: My God, why? Why have you allowed this? This is a personal question, as is also the question asked by those who by chance were not in that unfortunate railcar: Why not me? Why was I spared? How often we heard this question in the generation that experienced the war: Why did my comrades fall? Here again there will be only personal answers, for the question about divine providence is posed to each individual quite personally. Is God guiding my life? Back then, at that turning point in my life, when something happened to me that affected the rest of my life, was it chance, or did God arrange it?

The question becomes even more difficult when we introduce a distinction that is very important. It sounds somewhat philosophical, but it is very close to everyday life. Theology and philosophy distinguish between *physical* evil and *moral* evil. *Physical evil* befalls us in natural catastrophes or also in illness and, quite generally, in becoming and passing away. We live in a world in which everything is becoming and passing away. Nothing lasts, and all passing away is always connected also with dying, with being set aside, and that is an evil, but it is not a moral evil. It is the course of nature that leaves will fall in autumn, that death will do its work in nature, and that new life will come again in spring. This is part of the course of things. God created the world in such a way that it is not eternal and not already perfected but, rather, in progress. That is why, as long as this world exists, there will be becoming and passing away, growing and dying. *Moral evil* is something quite different and incomparably more momentous. This is found only in the world of men (and in the world of the angels), of creatures with free will, who with their freedom can decide either for or against the good and, therefore, can bring about and cause evil or else good. We will return again to this distinction. One thing that we can say already, of which nowadays we are perhaps too little aware: Moral evil is incomparably more serious than physical evil. Moral evil is much worse than an illness, even though an illness is an evil.

The big question, the big riddle, is not just the question of why God allows physical evil, sickness, and death, becoming and passing away, in his creation, but, rather, what about wickedness? Did God will it?—Certainly not. Does he allow it? Why does he permit it?

But let us return to the accident in Kaprun. Why did God permit this accident with its very personal consequences in the life stories of those who were affected and of their relatives and friends? One thing we know for sure: we will find the ultimate, certain answer to this big riddle only "in the next life". It is therefore helpful to look at the definition that the Catechism gives for providence: "We call 'divine providence' the dispositions by which God guides his creation toward this perfection" (CCC 302). God guides the world; God guides each of us toward his eternal goal. And we call these arrangements and this guidance his providence.

A second remark. In the eighteenth century, when a terrible earthquake in Lisbon killed 170,000 people—one of the greatest catastrophes in history—there was throughout Europe in that day a major discussion about God's providence. Did God allow that? The great cynic Voltaire (d. 1778) ridiculed faith in God's providence. But the wise old philosopher Immanuel Kant (d. 1804) said something very sobering: We must not blame God for this catastrophe when men build a city at a place located in an earthquake zone. Many catastrophes have human failure, carelessness, or negligence as their cause. The accident at the nuclear reactor in Chernobyl in 1986 came about through a series of indescribably careless blunders. There were so many earthquake victims in Turkey in 1998 largely because the construction

business there is so corrupt and they built cheap houses that
are not safe in an earthquake. The catastrophe with the Con-
corde jet on July 25, 2000, apparently can be traced back to a
small piece of metal that lay on the runway and punctured a
tire, from which pieces of rubber then flew into the engine.
That, in turn, led to a catastrophic explosion that sent 133
people to their deaths.

Divine providence does not "make up for" human failure. But God's providence does not abandon us when we
men fail. Even when human failure has terrible, even catastrophic effects, God does not abandon us. What, then, is
God's providence? Once again the definition cited before:
"We call 'divine providence' the dispositions by which God
guides his creation toward this perfection" (CCC 302). At
the end we will see, at the end we will understand how
God arranged everything, at the time when "God [will] be
everything to every one" (1 Cor 15:28), when "God . . .
will wipe away every tear" from our eyes, "and death shall
be no more, neither shall there be mourning nor crying nor
pain any more" (Rev 21:4); then God's love will triumph.
That is the assurance of faith we have when we believe in
divine providence. Through the Resurrection of Jesus, it
became certainty for us. God conquered death, as Christ
said to Dame Julian of Norwich (d. after 1416), a medieval
mystic: "All manner [of] thing shall be well."[1]

How God's Providence Works

Now, however, we come to the question: How does God
carry out his guidance and arrangements? How does he guide

[1] Julian of Norwich, *The Revelations of Divine Love*, trans. James Walsh, S.J.
(London, 1961), chap. 32, 99-100; CCC 313.

creation and our life to their perfection? When we look again at the Gospel, Jesus tells his twelve disciples that God's arrangements are *concrete and immediate*: "Even the hairs of your head are all numbered" (Mt 10:30), Jesus says. "Not one [sparrow] will fall to the ground without your Father's will" (Mt 10:29). "Fear not, therefore, you are of more value than many sparrows" (Mt 10:31). (This is not said to belittle love for animals but, rather, to point out the sure, firm guidance of God.) Elsewhere, Jesus says, "If a son asks his father for bread, will the father then give him a stone? How much more will your Father give you what you ask him for!" (Mt 7:9–11). The whole of Jesus' sermon aims to instill in our hearts trust in the fatherly kindness of God.

To believe in providence is, first of all, trust that God guides my life down to the smallest details. Nothing escapes his kindly hand. This deep trust should stand the test even in the most difficult hours. I remember the burial of a young man who was in a fatal accident. All around there were many tears. The only ones who were really composed were his parents. The attitude of those parents, who out of the convictions of their faith accepted this difficult trial, impressed me very much.

God's providence operates immediately. But it also *utilizes our providence*: the rescue workers who strive to help in a catastrophe; the people who answer an emergency call, offer consolation, carry out recovery efforts, or are just there for others—that is God's providence through the hearts and hands of men. It is impressive to see how many people spend days and nights making their hearts and their hands and their whole strength available in response to accidents and catastrophes like the one in Kaprun. That, too, is God's providence. When parents care for their children, that is God's providence through the parents' supervision. When children, once they are grown, care for their parents, it is God's providence through human providence. When we do our work well, methodically, neatly, and conscientiously, and provide for ourselves and for others, then that is God's providence through human providence. But at the same time we acknowledge: this human foresight and supervision, this care for others and for ourselves—that, too, is brought about by God. For God, indeed, moves my heart to help and to sympathize. And God gives me the strength of mind to see what to do and the strength of will to do it and to persevere. Thus God's providence always works directly and immediately, even when we work.

Very often this happens unawares. We are instruments of God's providence without knowing it. In my path through life, one telephone call was quite decisive. It determined which way I went at a fork in the road. I myself did not consciously notice it and did not consciously cooperate in God's plan. Today I know: that was God's doing. But we can also become conscious collaborators with God by doing good and fulfilling our duties, by our foresight, and we can also do this by suffering. Paul says it unambiguously: "In my flesh I complete what is lacking in Christ's afflictions" (Col 1:24). And we can cooperate through our prayer. We can help and collaborate in God's providence by asking him to do whatever his will, his plan, is and by collaborating in his work by our petitions.

Bringing Good Even out of Evil

The big question remains: What about evil and wickedness? I recall once again the distinction between *physical* evil and *moral* evil. God permits physical evil. He created a world that is imperfect, in which there will always be suffering, sickness, and death, as long as it continues to exist. That is why we can say that suffering and sickness and even death have their place in God's plan of creation. Moral evil, however, is not willed and is not caused by God in the slightest way. The Catechism says this explicitly: "God is in no way, directly or indirectly, the cause of moral evil" (CCC 311). God does not want us to do evil. Nor does he bring about the evil in us, although he gives us the freedom to do evil. God gives us reason, will, and strength and, consequently, the possibility of misusing them, too. But he does not bring about this misuse. God is not the cause of our sins. Yet in a mysterious way he derives good even from our sins. Even from our sins he can bring about good, even though our sins do not thereby become something good.

The Catechism mentions one example from the Bible, the story of Joseph (Gen 37–50). What Joseph's brothers did was without a doubt morally evil. They envied him and decided to kill him. Then they changed their plan, threw him into a cistern, and finally sold him to merchants who brought him to Egypt as a slave. In no way did God will this moral evil. They acted against God's commandment, sold their own brother, and lied to their father by claiming that a beast had torn him apart. And yet out of this moral evil, good came about. Joseph in Egypt, through the sufferings of his time as a slave, rose to become the vizier of the Pharaoh, and finally in that way he was able to save his brothers and his whole family from famine. At the end of the story of Joseph in the Book of Genesis, this becomes clear. Joseph tells his brothers, when he reveals himself to them: "It was not you who sent me here, but God. . . . You meant evil against me; but God meant it for good, to bring it about that many people should be kept alive" (Gen 45:8; 50:20;

cf. CCC 312). God can turn evil to the good, even our sins. Saint Augustine (d. 430) says it somewhere very beautifully: "For almighty God . . . , because he is supremely good, would never allow any evil whatsoever to exist in his works if he were not so all-powerful and good as to cause good to emerge from evil itself."[2] At the Easter Vigil we sing about the *felix culpa*, the "happy fault of Adam", which gained for us this Redeemer (*Exsultet*, Easter Proclamation). This is not to say that sin is blessed or good but, rather, that God in his incomprehensible goodness brings good even out of sin.

Trust in God's Goodness

Has there ever been a greater sin, a greater moral evil, than the murder of God's Son? The Catechism tells us quite clearly: We all put him to death, not only the Jews who handed him over then. All of us brought him to the Cross through our sins. The sins of all men are to blame for the rejection, the crucifixion, and the death of the Son of God (cf. CCC 598). And out of this, the greatest of all moral evils, God brought about the greatest blessing, the greatest of all goods: our redemption.

Evil itself does not thereby become good. But God in his goodness works good even out of the evil that we do. Saint Paul says: "We know that in everything God works for good with those who love him" (Rom 8:28). This is trust in divine providence. Of course we must admit: we cannot look over God's shoulder, so to speak, and see what is in the cards so as to comprehend his providence exactly. Why he arranged this in such and such a way, we will understand only at the end, in the next world, when God is "everything

---

[2] Saint Augustine, *Enchiridion* 11, 3 (PL 40:236); CCC 311.

to every one" and when we shall "see him face to face". Now our insight always remains fragmentary. Let us beware of saying that an accident like the one in Kaprun was God's providence. God permitted it. But what this accident means in the life of individuals, we can only accept in faith.

I would like to conclude with a passage from the Gospel of Luke that gives us much food for thought: "There were some present at that very time who told [Jesus] of the Galileans whose blood Pilate had mingled with their sacrifices" (Lk 13:1). Catastrophic news from that time: Pilate, the cruel governor appointed by the Roman Empire, had several Galileans killed in the temple, while they were offering sacrifice—a terribly bloody deed. They describe this to Jesus and thereby ask him: What is this supposed to mean? Why did such a thing happen? Then Jesus says to them: "Do you think that these Galileans were worse sinners than all the other Galileans, because they suffered thus? I tell you, No; but unless you repent you will all likewise perish" (Lk 13:2–3). And then Jesus adds another story, which was also a headline at that time, a catastrophe. The tower of Siloam collapsed and buried eighteen people under it. Jesus says: "Those eighteen upon whom the tower in Siloam fell and killed them, do you think that they were worse offenders than all the others who dwelt in Jerusalem?" And again the answer: "No; but unless you repent you will all likewise perish" (Lk 13:4–5). Is that perhaps the very personal question that Kaprun, too, has to ask us?

IV

"Salvation in No One Else . . ." (Acts 4:12)
The Uniqueness of Jesus Christ

> Great indeed, we confess, is the mystery of our religion.
> We praise you, Lord!
> He was manifested in the flesh. / We praise you, Lord.
> Vindicated in the Spirit. / We praise you, Lord.
> Seen by angels. / We praise you, Lord.
> Preached among the nations. / We praise you, Lord.
> Believed on in the world. / We praise you, Lord.
> Taken up in glory. / We praise you, Lord.
>
> (Cf. 1 Tim 3:16)

The motto of the Holy Year 2000 was: "Jesus Christ, the same yesterday, today, and always." This catechesis intends to take up once again this very topic, the central theme of the Holy Year: "There is salvation in no other name but the name of Jesus" (cf. Acts 4:12).

We profess the uniqueness of Christ. He is "the way, and the truth, and the life" (Jn 14:6). But we profess this in an age in which we are becoming increasingly aware that there are plenty of religions and that we encounter them in our everyday life together. In broad sectors of Europe, our Islamic fellow citizens already form the second-largest religious community, and in many parts of the world Christians are a small minority. And yet, in the midst of this multiplicity of religions, we profess that Jesus Christ is the only Mediator. There is salvation in no one else.

Believing and Asking

This catechesis is meant above all to edify, to strengthen faith, to encourage us in our faith. Yet questions are part of our faith journey, too. When we look into the Bible, how often we encounter people asking questions, even the Mother of God, who asks, "How can this be?" It is not forbidden to ask questions. Someone who goes along all too unquestioningly, even on the journey of faith, is in danger of being unable to answer when others ask him to give an account of his hope. We are still on the journey of faith, and it is a journey that has much that is obscure, too, even if our faith itself is firm and certain, as we shall see. We are not yet in the beatific vision, where God will be the answer to all our questions and where he will wipe away all tears. We are still confronted with many big riddles and questions, and we must not push them aside. They can even help us to make progress and to go deeper. In the Gospel we see how Jesus often leads people into a deeper understanding precisely through the questions that are posed to him and that he himself also poses, and thus he helps them to live out their faith better. Because these questions, after all, do not originate merely in the head. They are questions in our life, too. They can help us to become better acquainted with Christ, to learn to love him better and to experience more profoundly why and how he is *our* Savior, *my* Redeemer, so that we experience what Saint Paul did: "[He] loved *me* and gave himself *for me*" (Gal 2:20). The questions of life can lead us to the point where each of us can also say that about himself.

So this catechesis is therefore supposed to invite us, on the one hand, to a deeper, more complete faith but, also, to help us so that we can better address and perhaps also find answers to many questions that come up for us personally or that others ask us.

Peter and John before the Sanhedrin

Let us start with a passage from the Acts of the Apostles: Peter and John before the Sanhedrin (Acts 4:1–22). After Easter and Pentecost, Peter and John went to the temple. Sitting at the "Beautiful Gate" is a beggar, who has been crippled from birth. He looks up at them, hoping to re-ceive money from them. Instead, however, something sur-prising happens. Peter tells him: "I have no silver and gold, but I give you what I have; In the name of Jesus Christ of Nazareth, rise and walk!" (Acts 3:6). And he is healed. This poor, crippled beggar experiences salvation.

Things like this happen not just in the Acts of the Apos-tles, as demonstrated by many reports from our day as well. At liturgies as well as at the yearly celebration of the Holy Name of Mary in the Vienna City Hall, we often hear tes-timonies, for instance from Jean Pierre Belly, a Frenchman, who in Lourdes was cured of a hopeless, serious illness. I am also thinking, though, of experiences of inner healing, especially of healing from unbelief or of conversion to Jesus Christ. I recall here in particular a colleague, my revered teacher, the aforementioned Father François Paul Dreyfus, who was of Jewish descent, who after his baptism became a Dominican and who was able to describe movingly how it was for him, how he discovered Jesus as the Messiah of Israel, as the Savior. These are experiences of salvation like the one that this cripple had near the "Beautiful Gate" at the temple in Jerusalem.

Peter and John are brought before the Sanhedrin, the

supreme council, where they are forbidden to speak about this name of Jesus. But they say, "We cannot but speak of what we have seen and heard" (Acts 4:20). They say that it was the name of Jesus of Nazareth that healed that crippled man (Acts 4:10). And to emphasize this once more, they say, "And there is salvation in no one else, for there is no other name under heaven given among men by which we must be saved" (Acts 4:12). Jesus Christ is the only Savior and Redeemer. If someone says that today, especially considering the many religions of the world, among which Christianity is just one: Does it not sound arrogant? Does that not imply that all other religions are hopeless, if there is salvation only in the name of Jesus, if one can be saved only in this name?

Does that not lead to a terrible sort of intolerance? Would it not be better to moderate our claim, so to speak, so that people do not confront each other intolerantly, so that they do not fight each other, and so that coexistence does not ultimately become impossible? Frederick II of Prussia said this in his own inimitable style: "Everyone should become holy in his *façon* [French for 'fashion']." Everyone should have his own religion, the way he likes it—that is the very widespread opinion today. Many people, surely even among us Catholics, consider a claim like the one formulated here by Peter and John to be intolerant and totally unacceptable.

If we look a bit beyond Europe, then this question becomes even more dramatic. I remember a stay in India, that immense subcontinent which now accommodates a billion people. Only 2.7 percent of the people there are Christians, of whom only some are Catholics, while the others are Anglicans or belong to other Christian denominations. How is this vanishingly small minority of Christians supposed to coexist alongside the old major religions found in India, especially Hinduism, Buddhism, and the somewhat younger

Islam, and to live with this saying: "There is salvation in no other name but the name of Jesus"? So it is understandable, too, that many theologians in India set about looking for another way in this regard.

Salvation Only in Jesus Christ

Dominus Iesus, the Declaration of the Roman Congregation for the Doctrine of the Faith, "On the Unicity and Salvific Universality of Jesus Christ and the Church" (August 6, 2000), which caused such a stir and so much controversy in the media, has to do with precisely this question. Many theologians tried to find another way so as to avoid this dilemma: How do we live as Christians with such a claim, that Jesus Christ is the only Mediator, when there are so many other great and ancient religions alongside and around us? So they hit upon the idea of saying: Jesus Christ is one manifestation of God among many others. Jesus of Nazareth, they say, certainly testifies in a special way to God, but only as one among many. In this way they try to show that there is salvation elsewhere, too, in Buddhism also, in Hinduism, and in the other religions.

We must ask ourselves this question and try to find an answer to it on the basis of our faith. I remember a stay in Bangalore in Southern India, a major religious center, where many Catholics live, too. There I was a guest at the national catechetical and biblical center, on a very nice campus with houses and a chapel with an open door in the middle. Even from some distance you can see through the open door a pillar with the Blessed Sacrament in the tabernacle. Every day, early in the morning, the secretary of the institute came in and, standing at a distance, made the gesture that people in India make toward God as a sign of reverence: She lifted her hand to her forehead and made a bow. I asked the director of the institute: "Is this secretary Catholic?" He told me, "No, she is a pious Hindu woman. But every time she comes in, she makes this gesture of adoration and reverence toward the tabernacle, toward the Most Blessed Sacrament."

What is the meaning of the fact that quite obviously in all religions there are people of genuine piety and faith? How do alert Christians in India experience this situation, and how do we live with this situation, when more and more often we find among us, nearby us, perhaps in the house next door, perhaps in the same apartment building, Muslim families who take the practice of their religion seriously and pray several times a day? How do we deal with it? What does it mean, then, for us to believe that Jesus Christ is the only Mediator?

Now there is yet another level on which this question especially arises: this is the more philosophical level, which, however, has practical consequences. Today there is a widespread opinion that has been found in philosophy for more than two hundred years now and which also exists as a popular idea, namely, that as a matter of principle there is no absolute truth. There are always only approximations. Everyone sees a bit of the truth, everyone has a little insight, a little refracted ray of the truth, but the truth itself transcends everything and is ultimately incomprehensible. Naturally this implies that there is really no religion that is the true religion. All religions supposedly try to approach the absolute, the infinite, the mystery of God, just as one can see a mountain from one side or the other; in each case it looks a little different. It is in fact the same mountain, but no two people see it in quite the same way.

So how do we deal with these questions, which neverthe-

less extend into the heart of our faith? Do we bring one message among many selected arbitrarily from the warehouse
of contemporary religious offers, or do we bring the message about the One in whose name alone there is salvation?
When we try now to address this dilemma, one thing is
clear in advance: with our understanding alone we will not
be able to resolve it. Nor will we be able to grasp it through
our human experiences alone. For by our own efforts alone
we attain no final clarity in this question. By our human
reason we can approach many things, but only God himself
can give us the answer to this question.

My faith in Jesus Christ, indeed, is based initially, not
on my own understanding, or primarily on my own experiences, but rather on the unconditional trust that I have
in God. I believe *you*, because you told me this. I believe
you, because you are God. Our faith in Jesus Christ, therefore, is not based on what we ourselves can discover, find,
or devise but, rather, on "what no eye has seen, nor ear
heard, nor the heart of man conceived, what God has prepared for those who love him" (1 Cor 2:9). No man could
think up the mystery we celebrate in the Christmas season:
that this Child in the crib is the eternal Son of God. No religion invented this, no man discovered this; God has revealed
this. If he had not revealed it, we could not know it or believe it.

To put it another way: we do not maintain on our own
authority that Jesus is the only one in whom there is salvation. That is not an arrogant claim of Christians who have
imagined something; rather, it is, as Paul says, "the mystery
hidden for ages and generations" that was unexpressed but
that God has now revealed (Col 1:26), so that we might accept it in the obedience of faith. "God sent his Son." This
mystery is the reason for our faith, which we celebrate at

Christmas; it is the reason why in the year 2000 we celebrated a Jubilee, a Holy Year: "God sent his Son." That is
not something that human wisdom devised but, rather, what
God revealed. "When the time had fully come, God sent
forth his Son", Paul says in the Letter to the Galatians (4:4).

No Other Way than Jesus Christ

We believe that "in many and various ways God spoke" to
men. So it says in the Letter to the Hebrews (1:1). Through
the prophets of the Old Covenant, God spoke to men.
Through their consciences, he has also always spoken to
men in their hearts. The Letter to the Hebrews goes on to
say: "but in these last days he has spoken to us by a Son"—
and now comes an unbelievable statement—"whom he appointed *the heir of all things*. . . . He reflects the glory of God
and bears the very stamp of his nature, upholding the universe by his word of power" (Heb 1:2–3). We believe that
this Child in the crib is the heir of all things, who through
his Word upholds the universe. This great mystery was not
thought up by men. But if it is true, then it has major consequences.

What does it mean if this Child is really the eternal Son of
God, who upholds the universe through his mighty Word?
A hymn from the Letter to the Colossians elucidates this a
little. Paul sings the hymn, and the reader can almost imagine how the congregation to which he sent this letter continued to sing it. It is a solemn passage. We almost have to
sing this hymn while turning toward the crib, and in doing
so we always have to say: We are saying this about the one
who became a little child!

> With joy, giv[e] thanks to the Father, who has qualified us
> to share in the inheritance of the saints in light. He has de-

livered us from the dominion of darkness and transferred us to the kingdom of his beloved Son, in whom we have redemption, the forgiveness of sins. He is the image of the invisible God, the first-born of all creation; for in him *all* things were created, in heaven and on earth, visible and invisible, whether thrones or dominions or principalities or authorities—*all things* were created through him and for him. He is before all things, and in him *all things* hold together. He is the head of the body, the Church; he is the beginning, the first-born from the dead, that in everything he might be pre-eminent. For in him all the fulness of God was pleased to dwell, and through him to reconcile to himself all things, whether on earth or in heaven, making peace by the blood of his cross. (Col 1:12–20)

If someone hears these words and simply tries to accept them in faith: "Yes, Lord, so it is; I believe, I trust that it is so", then it absolutely cannot be otherwise: this *One* is the Mediator of salvation for *all* mankind. Then there really is salvation in no other name but his. Now, one could say that Saint Paul was an Oriental, that he was inclined to exaggeration and let his imagination run away with him. Many charismatic groups experience this; when the praise service really gets started, then you can sometimes exaggerate a little, too. But what if Jesus himself said that? I do not venture to say that Jesus himself gets into a state of charismatic enthusiasm, but he does shout for joy. The biblical scholars call this the "jubilus Jesu". He exults: "I thank you, Father, Lord of heaven and earth"—he calls the Lord of heaven and earth "Father"—"that you have hidden these things from the wise and understanding and revealed them to infants" (Mt 11:25). When we look more closely, we see that "these things" are, above all, who Jesus himself is. This he has revealed to the little ones. Saint Luke adds that Christ rejoiced "in the Holy Spirit" (Lk 10:21).

Then Jesus says something that confronts us with the unconditional alternative—either it is true, or this man is crazy —"Yes, Father, for such was your gracious will. All things have been delivered to me by my Father; and no one knows the Son except the Father, and no one knows the Father except the Son and any one to whom the Son chooses to reveal him" (Mt 11:26–27). With that Jesus already says what he will say even more clearly in the Gospel of John, in his farewell address at the Last Supper: "No one comes to the Father, but by me." There is no way to God except through Jesus (Jn 14:6).

"Jesus Christ Is Lord"

But what does it mean, when we look around and see many religions? "No one comes to the Father, but by me." Right before that, in response to the question of Thomas, "How can we know the way?" Jesus replies, "I am the way, and the truth, and the life" (Jn 14:5–6). What man can say such a thing: "I am the way, and the truth, and the life"? We could go on for a long time now finding similar passages in the Gospel, where Jesus so astonishingly and matter-of-factly speaks about himself in a way that confirms what Peter and John then said before the Sanhedrin: "There is no other name under heaven given among men by which we must be saved" (Acts 4:12).

Annemarie Schimmel [1922–2003], the great expert on Islam, wrote a very beautiful book with the title *And Mohammed Is His Prophet*. The subtitle reads: *The Veneration of the Prophet in Islamic Piety*. In it, this great scholar, who for a long time was a professor at Harvard University and is now retired, describes how Mohammed is honored and loved in Islam, how the prophet's life is recounted in all its details, how it has been embellished, indeed, how people simply love the prophet. Annemarie Schimmel says that it often is very painful for Muslims to see that Christians have so little understanding of the fact that they love Mohammed. If we venture—with the utmost caution—to compare Mohammed and Jesus, then I think I can say that Mohammed would never have dared to say about himself: "I am the way, and the truth, and the life", for Mohammed understood himself to be a prophet. And none of the prophets of the Old Testament ever dared to say about himself: "I am the way, and the truth, and the life."

I was in Sri Lanka and there had the privilege of experiencing one of the major feasts of popular Buddhism. I was also able to visit the national shrine, the temple in Kandy in the center of the country, to which pilgrims from the whole island, and also from India and from faraway places, travel in order to venerate there a most precious relic that reminds them of Buddha. A tooth of Buddha is preserved there and is carried through the city in a solemn procession with many elephants. I witnessed this procession; it is very impressive. Here, too, one sees this popular, profound love for Buddha, for his life. There are many stories from his life that are recounted, that remind people of him—and yet, and rightly so, no Buddhist would compose about Buddha the hymn that Paul handed down to us in the Letter to the Philippians, the hymn that we pray on Saturday in the Liturgy of the Hours, at Evening Prayer, which confronts us again with this stupendous question: How is it possible to speak in this way about a man, about a child in the crib? In the hymn in Philippians we read:

Have this mind among yourselves, which was in Christ Jesus, who, though he was in the form of God, did not count equality with God a thing to be grasped [literally: did not cling to it as though to plunder], but emptied himself, taking the form of a servant, being born in the likeness of men. And being found in human form he humbled himself and became obedient unto death, even death on a cross. Therefore God has highly exalted him and bestowed on him the name which is above every name, that at the name of Jesus every knee should bow, in heaven and on earth and under the earth, and every tongue confess that Jesus Christ is Lord, to the glory of God the Father. (Phil 2:5–11)

Try sometimes to listen to that with the ears of a believing Jew. When we look in the Old Testament, precisely the same thing is said as a statement about God: "For I am God, and there is no other. . . . 'To me every knee shall bow, every tongue shall swear'" (Is 45:22–23). In Acts 4:12 Peter says the same thing about Jesus: "There is salvation in no other name but Jesus."

If that is true, then there really is no other name in which salvation is granted to us, then Jesus is "the way, and the truth, and the life", then he is God's definitive Word. In Jesus, God has told us everything and given us everything. Naturally for the rest of our lives we will not cease comprehending this wealth ever more profoundly. We will never reach the end of it. We can never say: I have grasped it completely. But we can and must say in faith: "in [him] are hidden all the treasures of wisdom and knowledge", as Paul says in the Letter to the Colossians (2:3). He even says: "In him the whole fulness of deity dwells bodily" (Col 2:9). In this little Child dwells the whole fullness of deity in the flesh. No other religion ever said that. That does not mean that we Christians in and of ourselves are better or more pious than other people. Jesus often said, "not even in Israel have

I found such faith", for example to the Roman centurion in Capernaum, a pagan (Mt 8:10). But it is granted to us to know, to believe, and to proclaim that in no other name is there salvation but the name of Jesus. He is Truth in person. He is Life in person.

Now, of course, someone could object: That may be true in itself. We believe that God sent him, that Jesus is "true God and true man" (Council of Chalcedon, 451). But we poor, bungling, half-blind men—actually we always grasp only a tiny fragment of this truth. Can we ever say that we have grasped it completely? If he is the Truth, this does not mean that we have the truth, not by a long shot. How can we be so arrogant as to say to other people: We have the truth, and we can tell it to you? We know the way, and we can show it to you? Is it not true, after all, as many say today, that all religions are basically an attempt to grasp the incomprehensible mystery of God, to draw near to him, even though he became man in Jesus Christ? But not one of us can maintain that he has really grasped it. Is it not in fact just as the widespread spirit of the age assumes: that fundamentally all religions are relative; that each has a bit of the truth? That all of them are basically human attempts to draw near to God, yet God remains incomprehensible?

That We Might Become Children of God

I think that we still have to take one last step, a very decisive one. I will cite once again the Letter to the Galatians, where Paul so very personally puts his encounter with Jesus Christ into words:

> But when the time had fully come, God sent forth his
> Son, born of woman, born under the law, to redeem those

> who were under the law, so that we might receive adoption as sons. And because you are sons, God has sent the Spirit of his Son into our hearts, crying, "Abba! Father!" So through God you are no longer a slave but a son, and if a son then an heir. (Gal 4:4–7)

This is, I think, the decisive point: God sent his Son; he placed everything in him. All mysteries, all knowledge, all wisdom, all salvation is in his Son. And he made us his children. He placed it in us, also. John says it: "We [are] called children of God; and so we [really] are" (1 Jn 3:1). God gave us a share in his life. He put us on a par with Jesus. He made us, so to speak, blood relatives with him. We have become members of his Body.

I return once again to the Letter to the Colossians. There we read: "For in him [Christ] the whole fulness of deity dwells bodily." Then Paul adds: "And you have come to fulness of life in him" (Col 2:9–10). God became man, in order to unite himself with every man. Those who have been incorporated into Christ through baptism have become heirs with Christ, are sons and daughters of God. We really are children of God. We can grasp this only in faith, but in faith we can really assume it. If we take this seriously, then it does mean that our knowledge of what God revealed to us through his Son is genuine. John, the aged apostle, tells his congregation, which consists of very simple people: "You have been anointed by the Holy One", that is, by the Holy Spirit, "and you have no need that any one should teach you; as his anointing teaches you about everything" (1 Jn 2:20, 27).

For me one of the most powerful experiences of our faith is the fact that the very simple believers are the ones who grasp the mysteries that God revealed in Jesus. I have a friend whom I used to meet for several years in a prayer group in

Switzerland: a simple gardener, a man of deep prayer. At that time I was already a theology professor and was preparing my lectures on dogmatic theology. My dear friend said to me: "Even I can explain these mysteries to you." He had not studied theology. But he knew what the mystery of the Eucharist was, the mystery of grace, the mystery of new life in Christ, and he could testify to it in very simple words, because through Christ he had become an heir, a child of God, a son of God, and because the fullness of truth had been granted to him through Christ in the Holy Spirit.

In the twentieth century, there were more martyrs than ever before in the history of mankind. All these martyrs exist to testify to us that it is possible for very simple people to stand up for the truth of the faith, for the rightness of the way that Jesus has pointed out, even to the point of giving up their lives. Therefore, it is not true that nobody can really know anything and therefore everything is relative. In the Gospel, Jesus gave us clear instructions, clearly showed us a way, and he gave us a share in his wisdom through the Holy Spirit. When I think of [Blessed] Franz Jägerstätter (d. 1943): this simple farmer from Upper Austria knew things. Although he had not studied, he saw through National Socialism. He was able to distinguish lies from truth. Everything was not relative. He clearly recognized that National Socialism lied and that the Christian faith showed him the way of truth.

God Wants All to Be Saved

Now, what about those of whom we were speaking, the Buddhists, the Hindus, the Muslims, those who perhaps have never heard of Jesus or only remotely? Is there no salvation for them, if he is the only One in whom there is salvation? Paul says: "God . . . desires all men to be saved and to come to the knowledge of the truth" (1 Tim 2:4). God wants everybody to be saved. Moreover, he wants us to know the truth, because error does not save. Every man seeks the truth. As Christians, we have the commission to carry the light of truth that has been granted to us into this search and to bring the light of revelation and truth to those who are seeking the truth.

A word to those who have never heard about Jesus: " 'I was hungry and you gave me food. . . . I was naked and you clothed me. . . .' 'Lord, when did we see you hungry and feed you, . . . or naked and clothe you? . . .' 'As you did it to one of the least of these my brethren, you did it to me' ", says Jesus at the Last Judgment (Mt 25:35–40). This is true for all people, whether or not they knew him on earth. Then he will be the reward for all the good that was done by those who did not yet know him.

V

The One Church and the Many Denominations

"Saul, Saul, why do you persecute me?" (Acts 9:4). Paul is traveling on the road to Damascus to track down the Christians and to bring the disciples of Jesus, whom he is persecuting, before the Sanhedrin in Jerusalem. Then he sees a light that blinds him and hears a voice that calls to him: "Saul, Saul, why do you persecute *me*?" Saul is persecuting the disciples of Jesus, and Jesus, the Risen One, calls to him: "I am Jesus, whom you are persecuting" (Acts 9:5). No separation can be made, therefore, between Jesus and his disciples. He is one with his disciples. Anyone who persecutes them, persecutes him; he who hears them, hears him (cf. Lk 10:16). That is to be the subject of this catechesis. It is about the community we call "Church", about which we believe that it is one, the one, holy, catholic, apostolic Church. At the same time, we ask ourselves the unavoidable question: What is the significance of the fact that there are so many denominations? *Dominus Iesus*, a document of the Congregation for the Doctrine of the Faith in Rome, which was published with the Holy Father's approval, deals with the topics of the previous catechesis and of this one: the uniqueness and the salvific universality of Jesus Christ and of the Church. The last topic was the uniqueness of Jesus Christ; in the following remarks, we wish to turn to the second part: the one Church and the many denominations.

The Church of Jesus Christ

The goal of this catechesis is above all the growth of our love for the Church, so that it takes deeper root, as it were, so that we may grasp more profoundly and more broadly with our understanding but also with our heart how beautiful the Church of Jesus Christ is. It will discuss the fact that the Church is the Body of Christ: He is the Head, and we are the members (cf. 1 Cor 12:12–31a; Eph 4:7–16). When the members are persecuted, then the Head is persecuted, too: "Saul, Saul, why do you persecute me?" It will discuss the fact that Jesus, who is the Head of this Body, enlivens this Body, that it lives in him and by him. It will discuss the fact that the Church is also called the Bride of Christ, and is indeed that, and also that there can only be one Body of Christ. He does not have many bodies but, rather, many members in this one Body and, naturally, only one Bride, not many brides. It will discuss the fact that Jesus has given this Bride an inexhaustible wedding present, a treasure that Jesus won for her on the Cross, that he handed over to her and upon which she will draw until the end of time. This treasure will never be exhausted, the treasure of Jesus' love, which he handed over to the Church, his Bride. He will always care for this Church as his Body and his Bride. He will nourish her, will give her everything she needs until the end of time.

But when we look around a little, then it looks quite different. In February of 2000, I was in Nigeria, in Ibadan, a city with one or two million inhabitants—no one there knows, either, how many residents Ibadan has; it is an ocean of huts and little houses. As we were riding through the streets there, the archbishop showed me a house and said, "There is a church on each story." Each story had a balcony on which

a different church name was written: "Full Gospel Church",
"Mount Sion Church", "King David Church", and many
others. In Africa they call them "mushroom churches", because they spring up from the ground like mushrooms. Are
they all Churches? Rome says: No. They are "not Churches
in the proper sense", as it says verbatim in the Roman document, and there has been a lot of controversy over that.
Rome says in this document: although "those who are baptized in these communities are, by Baptism, incorporated in
Christ and thus are in a certain communion, albeit imperfect, with the Church", they are nevertheless "not Churches
in the proper sense".[1] That was said about the Protestant
churches, also, which left many people feeling very con-
cerned and hurt. Some assumed that there was great arrogance in this formulation of the document. How can the
Catholic Church maintain that other ecclesial communities
are not Churches in the proper sense?

Once again: Christ surely wanted there to be only one
Church. He gathered men into the one people of God, to
which he himself belonged as a Jew, and the Father sent
him to renew that people, to gather men even beyond the
boundaries of Israel into the one people of God, into the
one family of God. Christ willed *his* Church, and she can
only be *one*. To Simon Peter he says at Caesarea Philippi:
"You are Peter, and on this rock I will build my Church"
(Mt 16:18). This saying stands and is valid. "I will build
my Church on this rock." But what has become of her? An
endless series of divisions. In Iran, which is today a largely
Islamic country, Christianity was once very powerful. Today little groups of Christians live there, separated from one

---

[1] Congregation for the Doctrine of the Faith, Declaration *Dominus Iesus*
on the Unicity and Salvific Universality of Jesus Christ and the Church (August 6, 2000), 17.

another, a sad situation. Let us go to Jerusalem, to the place where Christ died for all mankind on the Cross. Let us go to Mount Golgotha, let us go down to the Rotunda of the Resurrection, to the tomb of Jesus, from which he arose; then we encounter there, too, a desolate picture of the divisions among Christians. There is haggling over every inch; everyone looks out strictly for his own rights at this, the holiest place in Christendom. What must the Muslims think about us at that place (even though they themselves are not unified)?

How are we doing in this regard? What does ecumenism look like in Austria? This has been a question again and again in recent times. Have we lulled ourselves with illusions that we have basically made a lot more progress already? Should we not soberly admit that we are by no means as far along as we thought and hoped? Or is it just the nervousness of the bishops or of Rome that has caused it to stall? What about ecumenism? This, too, will be discussed in this catechesis.

Jesus Willed One Church

But first, two preliminary remarks, which to me seem important. First: The Church is, as the Council says, a complex reality that "comes together" from visible and invisible elements, from human and divine components, from historical and supernatural structures. She is a complex reality made up of visible and invisible elements.[2] In this complex reality, which constitutes her mystery, she can be recognized only in faith. We can perceive much of the Church; we can see her in her visible appearances, in her greatness but also

---

[2] *Lumen gentium* 8.

in her weaknesses. Yet the real mystery of the Church can be seen only in faith.

A dear friend of mine, a confrere in the Dominican Order, borrowed an image for this from the Islamic world. He told this story about Afghanistan, where he lived for a long time. Formerly it was the custom there in arranged marriages that when the bride was first brought to the groom, who had previously been unacquainted with her, he was allowed to raise her veil in front of a mirror and thus saw her face for the first time in the mirror. Now, Father Serge de Beau-recueil, O.P., who describes this, says: That is the service that he performs there, to raise the veil so as to look into the face of the Church. Only faith can raise this veil. But in faith we see that the Church is incomparably beautiful. The Bride of Christ can be beautiful only if she is radiated by his light.

The second preliminary remark: I think that it is important to avoid a view of the multiplicity of Christian communities and Churches that is widespread today. There is the view that regards the Church of Jesus Christ as an ultimately invisible entity, something like an ideal goal, something toward which we are all making our way. Whatever ecclesial bodies [Kirchentümer] and churches in visible forms there may be, all that is, so to speak, only an approximation; they are approaches. We have the Catholic, the Evangelical-Lutheran, the Free-Church, the Orthodox, and many other ways, manifestations, expressions, and all are progressing toward this one goal of an ideal Church that will exist someday, when the imperfect passes away and the Kingdom of God is entirely realized. There is something very attractive about this idea, but unfortunately we must say that it is not right. There is something correct, naturally, at its core. Even now the Church is not perfect, she is on the road, she is a pilgrim Church. She will be perfect only when she has arrived completely in the Kingdom of God and is completely with the Father, when all men have reached their goal and hopefully will be gathered into their Father's house. Then the Church, too, will in fact be completely perfect. But that does not mean that now, during this time of pilgrimage in which we find ourselves, there are only fragments of the Church, so to speak, and some have a little of this aspect while others have some of that. No, the Catholic Church believes—and this is no doubt offensive—that the Church about which Jesus said to Peter, "You are Peter, and on this rock I will build my Church" (Mt 16:18), is realized concretely in the Catholic Church, in the Church that stays in communion with the successor of Peter. In her the fullness of the sacraments is realized, above all the Eucharist. Today that is no doubt a scandal. It was probably always so and is so quite especially today. But how does the Church understand this?

In the Gospel according to Luke (5:1–3), Jesus speaks to the crowd by the Sea of Gennesaret. There are so many people that he gets into a boat, so as to speak to the people from there. Luke notes that it was Peter's boat (Lk 5:3). That is surely not without symbolic significance for the Evangelist. Jesus speaks to us from the bark of Peter. Saint Ambrose (d. 397) said: "Ubi Petrus, ibi Ecclesia"—"Where Peter is, there is the Church." Of course Peter alone does not make up the Church, but without Peter the Church does not exist. "You are Peter, and on this rock I will build my Church." The Church of Jesus Christ is not an abstract idea, not an ideal goal; she is a reality, now, in human history. She is here, tangible, visible; she has a name; she has a leader, the man whom Jesus commanded: "Feed my sheep. . . . Feed my lambs" (Jn 21:15–17). That is why the Council says:

"This Church [of Jesus Christ] . . . subsists in the Catholic Church, which is governed by the successor of Peter and by the Bishops in communion with him."[3] The Latin expression for "subsists" is *subsistit in*. There has been a lot of debate in recent years over what this expression means: she is realized, she is visible, tangible, made a reality in the Catholic Church.

We cannot get around this stumbling block, and there is agitation about the Roman document, I think, not just because it is perhaps a bit harshly formulated, but because this is something offensive that completely contradicts the spirit of the age. But it is in keeping with the logic of the Incarnation, with God's logic. He became man, quite concretely, not in an idea, not in an ideal goal, but in Jesus of Nazareth in Galilee. At a definite point in time, God's Son became man. That is why the story of God's relations with mankind, the gathering of God's family from mankind, is for mankind a very concrete history. God became man. Jesus of Nazareth is the Son of God. The Church is his Body. Formerly people liked to say that the Church is the continuation of Christ's life, and no doubt there is truth in this expression. In the Church and through the Church, Christ is historically present in this time, in this world. Without the Church, even in her concrete form, Christ would perhaps be a historical personage whom people remembered, but he would not be the Present One, the One who is active now, who said, "I am with you always, to the close of the age" (Mt 28:20). He said this to the eleven apostles, and through them, who are the core, the beginning, the foundation stone of the Church, he is present in history to this day.

The reaction to *Dominus Iesus* is well known. It was above

---

[3] Ibid.

all the rebuke: "Typical: the Catholic Church considers herself the only one that sanctifies—what arrogance!" So a Church maintains that it is the realization of the Church of Jesus Christ, which means that it is the true Church of Jesus Christ. Is that not immensely arrogant? Here a taboo has been violated, a taboo of the spirit of our age, of political correctness, namely, through the statement that not only does truth exist but that it also and quite concretely has a place in history and that there is an authority that has something to say about the truth.

In preparation for my journey in Iran, I read the speeches that the Iranian president Khatami gave in Germany. I was surprised and also positively impressed by the clarity with which he speaks. The *Dialogue of Civilizations and Cultures* was the theme that he himself had also suggested to the United Nations as a theme for a calendar year and was accepted as the U.N. theme for 2001. Now this Muslim believer and president says: There is no dialogue without the question of truth. If there is no truth, then our exchange of opinions, our dialogue, is an arbitrary game. This, too, caused people in Germany to listen attentively: that a politician, a statesman, should say that today. If someone says today: "Truth exists, and it is knowable, even though we can only approach it and always see only perspectives, yet it exists and is fundamentally knowable", then very quickly you hear the accusation: "That is intolerant, that is even totalitarianism." That is the great suspicion, the general suspicion today: The Catholic Church is the last bastion of totalitarianism, because she claims to speak the truth. We must ask ourselves this question.

Truth, Unity, and Diversity

I would like to invite you now to set aside these problems for a moment and with a willing heart enter into the mystery of the Church with the eyes of faith. We profess in the Profession of Faith that the Church is one, the one, holy, catholic, and apostolic Church. I would like now, first of all, to speak about this unity of the Church and why we believe this and, secondly, to address the question of the multiplicity in the Church and, thirdly, the question: What actually constitutes this unity, what holds the Church together as a unity? And, finally, the painful question: How do these divisions come about, and what does it mean for the question about the one Church?

When we approach the Church in the perspective of faith, we begin with the triune God, as at the very top of many images over a high altar. The origin of the Church is one: God, who is *One and Triune*. The Council says: The Church is the people of God gathered together and unified by the unity of the Father and of the Son and of the Holy Spirit.[4] The one God calls men into the one family of God, the Church.

The Church is one in terms of her Founder. The Church has only one Lord, and the one Lord willed one Church. About this Church we believe that she is the sacrament of unity. The Council says that Christ gave his life in order to reconcile all mankind with God and to bring all men into unity.[5] This already happens symbolically, instrumentally, in the Church and through the Church.

[4] Vatican Council II, Decree on Ecumenism *Unitatis redintegratio* (November 21, 1964), 2.

[5] Vatican Council II, Pastoral Constitution on the Church in the Modern World *Gaudium et spes* (December 7, 1965), 78, 3.

The Church is one also in terms of her soul; she has a vital principle about which we speak much too little: the one Holy Spirit animates her. Just as the Church is the Body of Christ, the Fathers of the Church say, so the Church has a soul, which is the Holy Spirit. In the conciliar documents it says: "It is the Holy Spirit, dwelling in those who believe and pervading and ruling over the Church as a whole, who brings about that wonderful communion of the faithful. brings them into intimate union with Christ."[6] That is a faith perspective.

But faith is never demanded of us simply and blindly. We always receive all sorts of help as well. What faith teaches us to accept and to affirm is, so to speak, shown to us clearly through external and internal signs. I will mention three such signs for the Church. It is something marvelous to experience the Universal Church, the Church as one in all the multiplicity of peoples, languages, and cultures of the Universal Church. You can experience this in Rome, when traveling, or even in Vienna or in other major cities where there are so many foreign-language congregations from all over the world. In the one Church, the many peoples and languages are gathered. This is a perceptible sign of this unity, which comes from God, which the Holy Spirit breathes into the Church. Another strong sign of unity is the pope, even though the role of the pope, the mystery of his ministry, is a matter of faith. The fact that the pope is infallible, the fact that he has the assistance of the Holy Spirit in matters of faith and morals so as to show us the way of truth, cannot be proved mathematically; only faith can tell us that, and we can accept it only in faith. But one can perceive and experience the extent to which this ministry of Peter makes the

[6] *Unitatis redintegratio* 2, cf. CCC 813.

unity of the Church visible in a unique way. In the same dimension as the other signs but even more mysterious is the experience of the Eucharist. Even though we no longer have the same Latin language all over the world, wherever we may go to church, it is one liturgy, the one celebration of the Eucharist. It is the same faith, the same reality, and we experience the unity of the Church: a mystery of faith made visible.

Of course this unity is not uniformity; rather, it is unity in an incredible diversity, and this has been true from the beginning, from Pentecost. The many peoples who are in Jerusalem, who hear Peter and the apostles speaking in their own languages (Acts 2:11), already represent the whole Church in her diversity, as she lives to this day: the diversity of the gifts that each individual receives and that we all bring together, the diversity of the men who receive these gifts, the diversity of peoples, cultures, languages, the diversity of the living conditions and the ways of life—all this has its place in the unity of the Church (CCC 814). Of course, we know that this unity is always threatened, beginning in the parish community, in which there are conflicts, in the parish council, with the pastor and between groups in the parish, and on to the major tensions and conflicts between groups in the Church, between denominations, etc.

The Pain of Separation

What keeps all this together? What are the bonds of unity? What actually holds the Church together? Since the time of the Reformation, in which this question became very acute, three bonds have been mentioned that maintain the unity of the Church. They clarify the matter: the *bond of faith*, the same Profession of Faith; the *bond of divine worship*, of the sacraments—I mentioned this before: wherever we may go, we find the same liturgy, albeit in different languages, the bond of the sacramental celebration of the Church; and third, the *bond of apostolic succession*, which means the continuation of the episcopal ministry down through the centuries in the successors of Peter and in the bishops as successors of the apostles (CCC 815). These three bonds, the bond of faith, the bond of the sacraments, and the bond of the apostolic succession, keep the Church together. Where these bonds are missing or where one of these bonds is missing, something essential to the Church is lacking. Conversely, we can and must say (and this is now the really critical point): Where these things are realized, there the Church of Jesus Christ is realized. A passage from the Second Vatican Council puts this clearly into words, and even *Dominus Iesus* says nothing different but just reminds us of it once again. Precisely in the Decree on Ecumenism, the Council writes the following sentence:

> For it is only through Christ's Catholic Church, which is "the all-embracing means of salvation," that they [our separated brethren] can benefit fully from the means of salvation. We believe that Our Lord entrusted all the blessings of the New Covenant to the apostolic college alone, of which Peter is the head, in order to establish the one Body of Christ on earth to which all should be fully incorporated who belong in any way to the people of God.[7]

In the Catholic Church, therefore, all the gifts are on hand that Christ willed to give to his Church as means of salvation. What does that mean now for the others? Does it mean that the Catholic Church is the only true Church and

[7] *Unitatis redintegratio* 3.

all the others are nothing at all? How are we to understand it? Naturally, there would be the possibility of saying (and this temptation has occurred again and again): The Catholic Church is the one true Church, and therefore the others are, so to speak, nothing. But surely that is not true.

Let us observe, for instance, the Holy Father [John Paul II], how he relates to the other Christian Churches and communities. At the beginning of the Holy Year 2000, when he opened the Holy Doors at the Basilica of Saint Paul together with the archbishop of Canterbury and an Orthodox bishop, and on January 25, 2001, on the Feast of the Conversion of Saint Paul, when the same pope celebrated a worship service in Saint Paul's together with twenty-two Churches and ecclesial communities—not the Eucharist, but Evening Prayer —then there must be something there. This is evident from his actions: the others are not simply nothing.

What does it mean, though, when the Catholic Church says, indeed, in all honesty must say: The Church of Jesus Christ subsists in the Catholic Church? The Council puts it very beautifully: "Many elements of sanctification and of truth are found outside of [the Catholic Church's] visible structure."[8] This is true, first of all, about the other Christian Churches and communities, and then it is even true in the broader sense about other religions: "many elements of sanctification and of truth". With regard to the other Christians, the Council mentions, for example: "the written word of God; the life of grace; faith, hope and charity, with the other interior gifts of the Holy Spirit, and visible elements too [of the Church]".[9] The Council goes another step farther and says: The Spirit of Christ makes use of

[8] *Lumen gentium* 8.
[9] *Unitatis redintegratio* 3; cf. *Lumen gentium* 15.

these Churches and ecclesial communities as means of salvation.[10]

From the very beginning, the Church experienced divisions, even in Jerusalem, between the Greek-speaking and the Hebrew-speaking Christians. Very early on, Christendom was divided into Eastern and Western Christendom, and the divisions went even farther. In Persia, there was a flourishing Church, which exerted influence as far as China and Mongolia. It was separated from Western (Byzantine and Latin) Christendom. It became almost entirely extinct. How did these divisions come about? The reasons were, on the one hand, the errors and sins of men, but there were also external reasons why this Eastern Church in Persia could not have any contact with the Church of the West, and so they grew apart and slowly became estranged until a separation resulted. The Eastern Church and the Latin Church became increasingly estranged until they no longer understood each other. National, political, and ethnic differences came about and drove the Churches apart, but the fact that the Christian life was not lived out was also to blame. Would there have been a Reformation if the Church had been reformed in time, both head and members?

What happens when such divisions come about? Then those who go away always also take with them something of what is important, what belongs to the life of the Church; indeed, they rediscover much that perhaps was too little appreciated in the mainstream of the Church and must be brought to our attention again. Thus the Evangelical Lutheran Christians emphasized the Word of God anew, which had been far too neglected. What thereby left the unity of the Catholic Church, the Council says, are all gifts of the one Church

---

[10] *Unitatis redintegratio* 3; cf. CCC 819.

of Jesus Christ. These gifts emigrated, so to speak, and have built autonomous communities for themselves and, so the Council says, are "forces impelling toward Catholic unity", because they are actually gifts of the Church of Jesus Christ.[11] That is why, wherever the faith is lived out, there is a tendency toward unity, even though we are externally separated. The Council says this: that the desire to find our way back to the unity of all Christians is a gift of Christ and a call of the Holy Spirit.[12]

The Longing for Unity

Has not the Catholic Church also been so impoverished by division, therefore, that she can no longer make the claim that the Church of Jesus Christ subsists in her? Many think we must say: We have all in fact become poorer through these divisions, and none of the Churches fully realizes any more what it means to be Church. No, we cannot say that. We must in all humility but also in all clarity say: Despite the many mistakes that there have been in the Catholic Church, despite the sins of her members, the fullness of the means of salvation still subsists fully in the Catholic Church. She remains in continuity with the foundation of Jesus, because here Peter, here the successors to the apostles, and here the Eucharist, the mystery that Jesus gave to his disciples at the Last Supper, are realized. "You are Peter, and on this rock I will build my Church" (Mt 16:18). Even though Peter over the course of history again and again has also manifested his weakness, indeed, even his moral weakness—there have

---

[11] *Lumen gentium* 10.
[12] *Unitatis redintegratio* 4.

been very unholy popes—this saying of Jesus still stands and is valid. The Church of Jesus Christ subsists where Peter is.

Together with our seminarians, I was at Mass in the Holy Father's private chapel; I had the privilege of concelebrating. It stirs my faith and moves my heart every time I see him, about whom we can say in faith: "You are Peter." He is the successor. Yes, we make no mistake when we say that he is the *Vicarius Christi* [Vicar of Christ]. I know that the Church is there, because the Word of Jesus stands, is valid, and abides. I know that wherever the Eucharist is celebrated according to Jesus' commission, the Church is there. Now this does not mean that the Lord's Supper of the Lutherans is simply nothing in our view or even in their own self-understanding. If they celebrate the Lord's Supper in faith, they are correct in being convinced that Jesus is in their midst. "For where two or three are gathered in my name, there am I in the midst of them" (Mt 18:20). And yet we believe and must say it, without intending to hurt anyone: Something is lacking that is needed for the full reality of Church, precisely this communion with Peter and precisely this full reality of the Sacrament of the Eucharist.

Saint John Bosco (d. 1888) had a vision. We see it pictured in Turin in the Church of Mary, Help of Christians, which he built. Don Bosco sees the ship of the Church on a rough sea; Peter, the pope, stands dressed in white at the front of this ship; it is being attacked from all sides and is threatened by the storm. In the stormy sea stand two pillars. As the ship steers toward these two pillars, it comes into safe waters. On one of the two pillars stands Mary, Help of Christians, the image that Don Bosco revered so much, and on the other pillar is the Eucharist. This is the Church in her mysterious fullness and power. When we acknowledge this, we do not do so arrogantly or presumptuously but, rather, with the knowledge that something great and precious has been entrusted to us and also with the knowledge of how many spiritual gifts we can receive from one another and give one another, with the other Churches and ecclesial communities. There are many gifts of sanctification and of truth that are alive in the other ecclesial communities and Churches. I will mention only one example. On May 5, 2000, the Holy Father commemorated in Rome the martyrs of the twentieth century. It was an ecumenical celebration, because martyrdom is common to all Christians. There are countless Orthodox and Evangelical martyrs throughout the world. We sense that in this acknowledgment of Christ, this profession of faith, in the surrender of their lives by these witnesses to the faith, unity is already tangible and visible. This impels us toward the unity of Jesus Christ.

VI

The Signs and Miracles of Jesus

Miracles and Faith

Why this catechesis about the signs and miracles of Jesus? Should we not simply believe, without waiting for signs and miracles or staking everything on them? "Blessed are those who have not seen and yet believe", Jesus says to the apostle Thomas (Jn 20:29), who wants to see and touch. But what do signs and miracles have to do with faith? The following remarks are a reminder that miracles do not replace faith. But they can strengthen it. Miracles cannot produce faith. But when it is there, they can deepen it.

Another reason why this topic is important to me: Over and over it pains me to hear that miracles and the question about miracles are treated in a rather rationalistic way. One example, which was already used during the Enlightenment era, can be found today again and again. The miracle of the multiplication of the loaves, in which Jesus fed five thousand in a lonely spot with five loaves and two fishes, is explained by saying that Jesus' preaching moved the people so much that they suddenly began to think not only of themselves and of their hunger but also of their neighbor; they remembered that in fact they had all brought along brown-bag lunches, which they unpacked and shared. And behold, there was enough for everyone. Behind such Enlightenment attempts to explain away the miracles and signs of Jesus there is often a much more fundamental question: Is there such a thing in the first place as a divine intervention into history, into our lives? Or does everything instead run according to the iron laws of nature and perhaps also of history, without God ever directly interfering?

Somehow the question about miracles is always about the supernatural character of our faith as well. If I believe Jesus to be incapable of signs and miracles, if I call them into question, then how am I supposed to believe that Jesus is the Son of God, the Eternal One sent by God, who became man through the Holy Spirit, was conceived and born of the Virgin Mary, and ultimately rose from the dead? It is all too logical when, again and again, both are denied: that the signs and miracles of Jesus really exist and that he is the Son of God. I will mention one example, even though very often today in the exegetical literature it is taken to be self-evident. In the three so-called Synoptic Gospels—Matthew, Mark, and Luke—there is a discourse of Jesus about the end times. Shortly before his Passion, his suffering in Jerusalem, Jesus speaks about the things that will occur in the end times, among other things, about the end of Jerusalem also. Now we know that in A.D. 70 the Romans besieged Jerusalem, captured the city, and to a great extent destroyed it. The conclusion drawn from this and almost taken for granted is: If there is talk about the fall of Jerusalem in the Gospels, then this must have been written down after those events. That may be. But another question must also be asked: Could not Jesus have predicted something? Can this just be a matter of Jesus' prophecy? If you want to be scientifically correct, then at least this hypothesis cannot simply be ruled out. Do we really believe that Jesus was capable of supernatural deeds? That he foretold his Passion, as the Gospels tell us, and his Resurrection and perhaps the fall of Jerusalem, too?

I am anxious to treat the topic of the signs and miracles of

Jesus as a catechesis, that is, as something that will strengthen our faith. For the signs and miracles of Jesus are signs from above, signs that make visible the supernatural character of our faith. But how should we approach the topic? It is important to clear up a few preliminary questions, for in this matter a lot goes on in the preliminary questions. C. S. Lewis (d. 1963), the Anglican writer, to whom we owe a marvelous book about miracles, begins with an anecdote:

> In all my life I have met only one person who claims to have seen a ghost. And the interesting thing about the story is that that person disbelieved in the immortal soul before she saw the ghost and still disbelieves after seeing it. She says that what she saw must have been an illusion or a trick of the nerves. And obviously she may be right. Seeing is not believing.
>
> For this reason, the question whether miracles occur can never be answered simply by experience. . . . If anything extraordinary seems to have happened, we can always say that we have been the victims of an illusion. . . . It is therefore useless to appeal to experience before we have settled, as well as we can, the philosophical question.[1]

Wrong Ways in the Question about Miracles

There are several pitfalls in the question about miracles that we first must clear out of the way, so that we do not stumble into them. One such pitfall, for example, is the statement: People formerly had a more primitive view of the world than we do, a prescientific way of observing, and they considered many things to be "miracles" that today we can explain in entirely natural terms, either for medical reasons or

[1] C. S. Lewis, *Miracles* (1947; New York: HarperOne, 2009), 1–2.

as natural phenomena that could not be understood at that time. Thus, many of Jesus' miraculous cures could be explained quite naturally with our present-day knowledge of medicine.

Another pitfall: If miracles did happen, some say, then they would compel faith. Then you could not help but believe. One could by no means escape the necessity of believing. But that would be contrary to the freedom that God gave man. God forces no man to believe. Therefore, it cannot be the case that there are miracles that can be clearly proved to be such.

A third pitfall: The laws of nature are what they are. How is God supposed to break the laws of nature, which he himself gave to his creation? After all, that would contradict the order of his creation. He gives nature laws, and then he breaks them: Is that not a contradiction?

A fourth pitfall, which sounds quite different but can also be an obstacle: If God were to work today the miracles that he worked in Jesus' time or in the early Church, then our churches would be full; then everybody would believe. Let us try to remove these pitfalls so that we can examine this matter more closely.

Before we start, I would like to make one thing clear about myself personally. I do not want to require this of anyone and cannot do so. Personally, I believe—and, it seems to me, with good reason—that there is no miracle of Jesus about which I can say: It cannot have been like that. I do not dare to say that about any miracle of Jesus. From my perspective, I would consider that presumption. But if someone else sees things differently, please feel free. Formulated positively, I may respectfully say about all the signs and miracles of Jesus: Why should the Master not have done that? Multiplications of loaves as well as the many cures, walking on the sea, or the raising of Lazarus. Why should the Lord have not known the hearts of men? Why should he not have foretold future events? What strengthens me in this conviction is one very simple thing. For each one of the miracles and signs of Jesus that are reported in the Gospels, there are in the history of the Church numerous analogies, many parallel examples. When you look through the acts of canonization from the last two or three hundred years, which were drawn up very strictly according to the historical method, then for each one of Jesus' miracles you can find parallels in the lives of the saints. That is not a proof. It is interesting, however, to point this out. Obviously, the miracles of Jesus that the New Testament records are not isolated phenomena. And then there is another fact. Some people criticize the Holy Father for performing too many canonizations and beatifications. With the exception of the martyrs, a medically and theologically approved miracle is required for each beatification and canonization. In other words, without a "signature from above", "from on high", there can be no beatification or canonization. And the methods of testing are extremely rigorous—the theological tests are even stricter than the medical ones.

But this, too, must be clear from the start: miracles do not compel anyone to believe. I will say more about this in a moment. Nor do miracles break the laws of nature. I will say more about this, too. And miracles—this will be the last and perhaps the most important point in this catechesis—miracles always belong in a particular setting. They are not isolated marvels, some kind of strange occurrences, and they have nothing to do with "show business". They are signs of faith and signs for faith. Their "biotope", their habitat, is the life of faith. Miracles are at home there.

Miracles—Not a Medicine against Disbelief

I will begin with the difficult question: Do miracles compel one to believe? Again and again we can read this argument: If a miracle were ever proved, then it would compel people to believe. But that cannot be; that would contradict faith as a free act of the will. I will begin with a famous example. Alexis Carrel (d. 1944), a physician who won the Nobel Prize in 1912, witnessed a cure in 1902 in Lourdes. He writes about it: "I believe in miraculous cures, and I shall never forget the impact I felt watching with my own eyes how an enormous cancerous growth on the hand of a worker dissolved and changed into a light scar. I cannot understand, but I can even less doubt what I saw with my own eyes."[2] Alexis Carrel was an agnostic, an unbeliever. You might expect that he immediately fell on his knees and converted. But not until 1944, shortly before his death, did he become a Christian, forty-two years later. Miracles do not compel anyone to believe. I could relate a very similar incident from the life of my grandfather, which also took place in Lourdes. He, too, came to be reconciled with God and the Church only on his deathbed.

This is also true the other way around. Those who expect that everyone would come to believe if only they could witness enough miracles are deceiving themselves. There is a famous sermon by John Henry Newman (d. 1890). In 1830, while still an Anglican, he gave a sermon on the topic: "Miracles No Remedy for Unbelief". Newman starts from the observation that if miracles were to compel faith, then it would be incomprehensible why the people of Israel ceased

---

[2] Alexis Carrel, *Man: The Unknown* (London: H. Hamilton, 1935); translated into German as *Der Mensch, das unbekannte Wesen* (Stuttgart, 1936), 314.

to believe. He quotes from the Bible: "How long will this people provoke Me? And how long will it be ere they believe Me, for all the signs which I have showed among them?" (Num 14:11). Despite the miracles, they do not believe. And Newman refers in this sermon to the passage in the Gospel of John where the high priest says to the Sanhedrin: "'What are we to do? For this Man performs many signs. If we let him go on like this, every one will believe in him, and the Romans will come and destroy both our holy place and our nation.' . . . So from that day on they took counsel about how to put him to death" (Jn 11:47–48, 53). And so they say it quite openly: He works miracles. But they do not believe. On the contrary, they hate him. And Newman says: "Hard as it is to believe, miracles certainly do not make men better." Let that be a consolation to all who have not yet witnessed a miracle. "Miracles certainly do not make men better; the history of Israel proves it." Since Israel was no worse than other peoples, this must be due to the peculiar character of miracles and not to the wickedness of the Jews. "It was not that the Israelites were much more hard-hearted than other people, but that a miraculous religion is not much more influential than other religions." And from this Newman concludes: "the sight of miracles is not the way in which men come to believe and obey, nor [is] the absence of them an excuse for not believing and obeying."[3] This is of course the *Sitz im Leben* [existential setting] of this sermon by John Henry Newman. Many believers think that if there were only a few more miracles, as in biblical times, then faith would be much easier. I would like to quote another passage from this very moving sermon:

[3] John Henry Newman, *Parochial and Plain Sermons* (1891; San Francisco: Ignatius Press, 1997), 1611, 1613.

I ask, why should the sight of a miracle make you better than you are? Do you doubt at all the being and power of God? No. Do you doubt what you ought to *do?* No. Do you doubt at all that the rain, for instance, and sunshine, come from Him? Or that the fresh life of each year, as it comes, is His work, and that all nature bursts into beauty and richness at His bidding? You do not doubt it at all. Nor do you doubt, on the other hand, that it is your duty to obey Him who made the world and who made you. And yet, with the knowledge of all this, you find you cannot prevail upon yourselves to do what you know you should do. Knowledge is not what you want to make you obedient. You have knowledge enough already. Now what truth would a miracle convey to you which you do not learn from the works of God around you? What would it teach you concerning God which you do not already believe without having seen it?[4]

After these sobering words from the great and hopefully soon-to-be-canonized John Henry Newman, we can turn once again to the question: Why are there miracles? I would like to address two questions more explicitly now, first the question, the pitfall: Are miracles a breach of the laws of nature? And what about God's intervention? Does God interfere in the world when he works a miracle? The second area of inquiry will be: What meaning do miracles have, then, if they do not compel faith, indeed, do not even produce it, if they are not at all necessary for our salvation, either, if we already know anyway what we have to do?

[4] Ibid., 1614.

Miracles and Laws of Nature

Are miracles a violation of the laws of nature, of natural processes? First a preliminary remark: Laws of nature do not exist in nature. They exist only in our heads and in our books. Laws of nature are the conclusions we draw when we observe nature and determine that regularities exist in it. That is then formulated as a law of nature, for instance, gravity and the like.

But is there such a thing as divine intervention into nature, into natural processes? By our freely made decisions, originating in our mind, we can intervene in the course of nature, we can introduce something new into natural processes and thereby change them. C. S. Lewis says very beautifully: "Nature is an accomplished hostess" who accepts what we bring to it. We do not break the laws of nature when we act in nature. When the doctor gives a medicine or makes a surgical intervention, that is indeed an intervention, but it breaks no laws of nature; rather, it brings, so to speak, a new element, a new factor into the processes of nature. Of course, we know also that if these interventions are not in keeping with nature, if they are made brutally, then there is the danger of "violating" nature. Then we say, correctly, that nature "takes revenge". We are experiencing something of this sort today in a terrifying and dramatic way with all the consequences in the world of animals that have resulted from violations of nature. Bovine spongiform encephalopathy (BSE, "mad-cow disease") and all sorts of other phenomena are the consequences when man intervenes in a way that is not in accordance with nature. When chickens are kept in egg-laying processing plants, when animals are treated inappropriately, there should be no surprise when nature avenges itself. All this has its origin in man's freedom. It was first devised in the human mind and then accomplished by human hands, brought into the processes of nature.

God, too, can intervene in nature, of course, with one essential difference. We can shape and change nature and work with it. We can perhaps also misuse it, but always and only within the parameters of possibility that nature itself offers us. We can act only within the framework of what is given. The artist, too, can make forms only out of available material. With God it is different. He really can introduce something new into nature. But, first, let us stay for the moment with human action in nature. When a doctor tries to cure an illness, he can do nothing but mobilize the natural healing powers by medical, therapeutic, or surgical measures. But if the healing powers in the body are insufficient, when nature no longer can "manage" it, then even the doctor is powerless and has reached the end of his art. God's art is not at its end there. In his freedom, God can introduce into nature a factor that it does not have on its own. Because he is the sovereign Creator, who created all things out of nothing, he can also, for example, introduce into a sick body, as it were, a factor of reorganization, of re-information, which medicine can no longer offer. Medicine can only help and support. God can also intervene by creating anew. This supernatural factor is not a foreign body. It is not an invasion into the laws of nature and certainly not a violation of the laws of nature; rather, we might say, God re-informs, he reconstitutes what is already there in his order of creation. Nature is a good hostess and welcomes this action of God. She integrates it right away. What happens when a body is miraculously healed? The cause—God's sovereign, free, healing action—is supernatural, but the effect is completely natural. The healed organ, the organ freed from cancer, is again quite natural, is precisely this healed organ. In a miracle, God does not violate nature, as we do again and again; rather, he restores nature; in a supernatural way, he once again establishes it in its natural state.

Let us keep in mind this *supernatural factor*, as I would like to call it, when we discuss the even greater question of what spiritual miracles really are. Bodily miracles, after all, point beyond the visible to spiritual consequences in the life of souls. There are miracles in which souls are healed, and these are greater and even more mysterious than the healing of the body. There are miracles of conversion, when a heart is transformed, when something that seemed humanly impossible is granted by God: conversion, like that of Paul on the road to Damascus.

What Miracles Have Wrought

What sort of meaning do miracles have? We have seen that for faith they are not necessary; they cannot compel it or bring it about. Why, then, did our Lord work so many signs and miracles? Saint Augustine (d. 430) says very nicely in one passage: Signs and miracles, too, are a language. We must understand them; we must spell them out. The signs and miracles of Jesus have a very definite grammar. It is not just any arbitrary written code. Let us try to decipher a bit of Jesus' sign language. I will mention seven brief points in the grammar of our Lord's signs. From that we will see what he wants to tell us, what miracles have to say to us.

1. Signs and miracles are always found within a *religious context*. It is not just a matter of inexplicable phenomena.

We normally do not regard UFOs as miracles. I have still not seen a UFO. Yet I am acquainted with UFO-enthusiasts who staunchly maintain that they have seen UFOs and read thick books about them. UFOs may be marvelous things, but they are not miracles. Signs and miracles always have to do with what we hope to receive from God, help that we have prayed for, a sign from God that we have requested, an appeal for his gifts and his healing. That is why the signs and miracles of Jesus are always connected with faith. Not that they make faith, but they presuppose it. "All things are possible to him who believes", Jesus says to the father who asks for the healing of his child (Mk 9:23). Where this faith does not exist, Jesus cannot work miracles, not because he does not have the power, but, rather, because no room is made for it. In Nazareth, his hometown, where he runs up against so much opposition and unbelief, he works no miracles (Mk 6:5). In places where the people demand a sign from him so as to prove that he is the Messiah, he leaves them and gives them no sign (Mk 8:11-13).

2. Signs and miracles are found not only in a religious context but always in an *existential context*, as well. This is not a matter of theoretical questions of medical research, for instance, what happens to a carcinoma when a miracle occurs. It is always about a very specific need. "Lord, my servant is lying paralyzed at home, in terrible distress" (Mt 8:6); or the Syro-Phoenician woman who kept following Jesus and calling on him to heal her daughter (Mk 7:25-26); or the woman who was bent over and for eighteen years, as Jesus says, was bound by Satan (Lk 13:11); or the woman with the hemorrhage, who for twelve years had spent all her money on doctors in vain (Mk 5:25); the great need of the lepers, the blind, the lame; the inconsolable grief of the mother in Nain whose only son had died (Lk 7:11-12) —this need is the context in which the signs and miracles

of Jesus are found. Jesus speaks to this need: "I will it, be clean!" (Mk 1:41).

3. The signs and miracles of Jesus are always connected with ultimate *questions of meaning and faith*. People who have reached the limit in their life, who can no longer cope, whose distress is so great that they cry to God for help, as we read again and again in the Psalms, people whom no man can help any more: to them the Lord manifests himself as their Savior.

4. Jesus' signs and miracles have a definite "style", an *unmistakable, inimitable style*. Even the greatest skeptic will say that some miracles are a little more credible than others. The greatest fan of miracles will say about some miracles: Now that really is a little implausible. There are things like criteria for the credibility of miracles. For one thing, suitability: Does that fit Jesus? When, for example, bad boys mistreat the Child Jesus and to punish them he turns them into swine? That is not in the New Testament, but it is in an apocryphal gospel. We spontaneously say: That does not befit Jesus. Or when clay figures of birds are transformed into living birds (the Infancy Gospel of Thomas). This is a spectacular prodigy that does not belong with the miracles of Jesus. I admit that among the authentic miracles of Jesus I have a little more difficulty with the two thousand swine of Gerasa (Mk 5:11–13) than with the healing of blind Bartimaeus (Mk 10:46–52), which so touches our heart. The miracles of Jesus have a certain style. People say: He did all things well. The signs of Jesus are the interpretation of his goodwill toward mankind. They are signs that God is a friend of men, as Maurice Blondel once put it: "They make unusual kindness visible through unusual signs."

5. However much the miracles and signs of Jesus appeal to the heart and speak a philanthropic language, another essential feature of them is the fact that they *provoke opposition*,

not because Jesus proves therein to be good, but because they demand a response. They do not only appeal, they also challenge, they make a demand. The signs and miracles of Jesus are not just simple statements of God's goodness; they are also challenges to conversion. Hence they encounter opposition. They encounter the opposition of our laziness, which is unwilling to convert. For the healings and miracles of Jesus in fact point to something more important, the *conversion of the heart*, the healing of our sins. The miracles of Jesus mean to change our lives, and there is a lot of resistance to that. I often marvel at how easily UFOs are believed and how much difficulty people have in believing the miracles of Jesus. Probably for just this reason.

6. The signs and miracles of Jesus make a *demand on us*. They speak not only about something but about someone. They speak about Him. Not only does someone speak in them, but He gives us something. In his signs and wonders, Jesus manifests himself as the Savior. He already gives salvation now. He makes us whole.

7. With that I have arrived at the last characteristic of the signs and miracles of Jesus. They are signs of the goodness of God and his love for mankind. But among all the signs that Jesus performed, there is none greater than the sign of the Cross. Nowhere did he show his love for mankind as he did in the sacrifice of his life for us. That is why the Cross is the greatest sign. There is no opposition between the healing miracles of Jesus and the great healing and reconciliation of the world through the Cross.

8. We are at the end of this catechesis, but I must mention yet another point, not entirely coincidentally the symbolism of the eighth day. The miracles of Jesus are always advance signs of the Resurrection as well. When he straightens the woman who was bent over, when he heals the blind man,

then that is an anticipation of Easter. Then Easter already happens for those people. The signs and miracles of Jesus are signs of the Paschal Mystery of Jesus, of his Cross and Resurrection. That is why the next catechesis will be about the Resurrection of Jesus.

"The Lord Has Risen Indeed" (Lk 24:34) The Resurrection of Jesus— The Resurrection of the Dead

Christ is risen from all his torment.
Therefore we should rejoice; Christ wants to be
  our consolation.

Kyrieleis.

If he had not risen, the world would be lost.
Since he has risen, all that exists rejoices.

Kyrieleis.

Hallelujah, Hallelujah, Hallelujah. Therefore, we
  should all be glad.
Christ wants to be our consolation.

Kyrieleis.

[An old German Easter hymn]

The Resurrection of Jesus Today

"Christos voskrese!" "Christ is risen", so the Russian Orthodox greet one another throughout the Easter season. And
they reply: "Voistinu voskrese!" "Truly he is risen."

He is truly risen. Our blasé society says: Well? So what?
What has actually changed? What does that actually mean?
A miracle, just like many extraordinary events that occur!

Festus, the second successor of Pontius Pilate as Rome's
governor in Palestine, is responsible for a prisoner that his
predecessor, Felix, left behind for him in Caesarea. He does

not really know what he should do, and he writes to King Agrippa about this Paul; it is a matter of "certain points of dispute with him about their own superstition [i.e., the Jewish religion] and about one Jesus, who was dead, but whom Paul asserted to be alive". And Festus goes on to relate: "Being at a loss how to investigate these questions, I asked whether he wished to go to Jerusalem and be tried there regarding them" (Acts 25:19–20). Paul declined, and now Festus asks King Agrippa to help him in this difficult situation. Paul speaks, therefore, about a certain Jesus who died. That is obvious even for Festus, the educated Roman governor. He knows that his next-to-last predecessor, Pontius Pilate, had him crucified in Jerusalem. Paul now maintains that he is alive.

That means that there are people who say that he is risen, that he lives. His tomb is said to have been empty, and he reportedly showed himself to some people. But what about it? There are many strange phenomena in the world, about which people speak for a time, and then they forget them again. The world goes on, it keeps turning; the events basically remain the same.

So it has been to this day. The most solemn feast day of Christians has evidently become an object of ridicule for our pleasure-seeking society. Often the programs on TV channels show little or no consideration for Good Friday. Contemporary magazines do their part with caricatures that make vulgar fun of the Church, Christianity, and even Christ. It is unthinkable that such a thing could happen at Ramadan or at Yom Kippur.

What is the significance of this trivialization of Easter to the point of Easter bunnies, on the one hand, and, on the other hand, the mockery of the Christian faith that is carried on so openly? Even back in Athens, the citizens had no idea what to make of the message of the Resurrection. When Paul strove to present the message of Jesus to the Athenians in the Areopagus, he spoke first about the Creator. Then when he spoke about a man approved by God, about Jesus of Nazareth, whom God had awakened from the dead, the Athenians no longer wanted to listen to him. Some mocked him to his face, while others said somewhat more politely: "We will hear you again about this" (Acts 17:19–34).

On the Road to Emmaus

The honest question that needs to be posed to us, to our Church today, to our ecclesial existence, and to our life as Christians is: What difference would it make if the tomb had not been empty? There are quite a few biblical scholars who consider this rather irrelevant. The Christian faith could by all means continue to exist even if the tomb in Jerusalem had not been empty, so they say over and over again. This opinion is widespread. Why, in fact, is it so important that he really rose in the flesh and that, therefore, the tomb is really empty? What does it mean that he lives on and not just in memory, that this "He is truly risen" is the core of our message? And if that is so, how does it change our lives?

In our ecclesial situation today, are we not like the two disciples who, disappointed, are going back from Jerusalem to their hometown of Emmaus? Granted, they did hear all sorts of things. Women supposedly had seen the tomb empty and an angel who spoke about Jesus being risen. The apostles had considered the women's reports to be empty talk. Thereupon some of them went and allegedly had found it so, but Jesus they did not see (Lk 24:1–12). The two men were disappointed as they were walking to Emmaus.

For two hundred years now, historical criticism, but especially the world view that comes from the Enlightenment, has tried to persuade us that the Resurrection appearances were the result of autosuggestion. Thus even today we can read, for instance, the theory that the disciples were cowardly, ran away, and betrayed their Master. Under the influence of a guilty conscience, their imagination was inflamed, so to speak. Therefore, he just had to live on, his cause had to continue, it could not simply be all over. In order to escape from this situation, they allegedly "invented" the Resurrection and "imagined" the appearances. Of course, that then makes it difficult to explain, if one takes it seriously, something like Paul's report that the Lord appeared also to five hundred disciples at once. Did they have a mass hallucination? But the fact remains that the Enlightenment and practically the last two hundred years have been trying in one form or another to make us believe that it was all pious imagining. And, unfortunately, this doubt is deep-seated among us, too; sometimes preaching is even influenced by it.

When you look at the Gospel passages and put them side by side, there are at first glance many contradictions. According to Luke the Evangelist, everything happens in Jerusalem, whereas Matthew and John shift the appearances mainly to Galilee. How can this be explained? On the basis of these at least apparent contradictions, many conclude that there is no historical truth but, rather, a symbolic truth behind them. The cause of Jesus goes on; we have not forgotten him; we continue to think about him and strive to carry on his concerns. But can that really be the explanation?

We could make an effort now to examine the Gospel accounts individually and to ask to what extent they are historically reliable. This can demonstrate a lot. I am convinced that the Gospel accounts about the Resurrection of Jesus, about the appearances of the Risen One, bear the marks of reliable reports and do not reflect the hallucinatory fantasies of overheated tempers.

However, true to our catechetical method, I would like to go another way. What happened to the disciples on their way to Emmaus should happen in a catechesis. At the end of their journey, when Jesus broke bread for them and then withdrew from their sight, they stood up and said, "Did not our hearts burn within us while he talked to us on the road, while he opened to us the Scriptures?" (Lk 24:32). Like them, we too have a good catechist: Jesus himself is with us along the way and reveals to us what Scripture says about him. He is the catechist who walks with us in our lives. He is the catechist who says to doubting Thomas, "Put your finger here, and see my hands; and put out your hand, and place it in my side; do not be faithless, but believing" (Jn 20:27). Jesus opens up for us the meaning and opens our ears and enkindles our hearts. And just as he rebuked the disciples' unbelief then, so too today: "He upbraided them for their unbelief" (Mk 16:14). Why are you so slow to understand? Why are your hearts so heavy? Therefore, he would like to guide us, too, and we want to be guided by him.

Resurrection Catechesis on Easter Night

To believe in the Resurrection is not something isolated but means, first of all, to believe in *Him*, to believe in Jesus Christ, whom the Father sent to us. Believing means entrusting ourselves to him and accepting what he has shown us, walking the path onto which he has guided us. The Resurrection of Jesus is not scientific data that we investigate and report neutrally, the way a scientist conducts a physics or chemistry experiment. It is the high point of a journey, and we ourselves are invited to go along.

On the road to Emmaus, Jesus speaks with the disciples. They do not yet recognize him, they do not yet know that it is he, this stranger who is walking with them, listening to them, and asking them: Why are you so sad? What are you talking about along the way? (Lk 24:17), and who then says to them: "Was it not necessary that the Christ should suffer these things and enter into his glory?" Then we read, "And beginning with Moses and all the prophets, he interpreted to them in all the Scriptures the things concerning himself" (Lk 24:26–27). What did he tell them along the way? It was the most important catechism class in human history. Unfortunately, the two disciples had no tape recorder on hand. They did not write it down, either, they took no minutes. We do not know what he said to them along the way. Just like the first two who had followed Jesus, back then at the place where John was preaching at the Jordan, when Jesus had turned around and said, "What do you seek?"—"Rabbi, where are you staying?"—"Come and see." "They came and saw where he was staying; and they stayed with him that day" (Jn 1:38–39). They, too, unfortunately, wrote nothing down of what he told them. The first conversation with Jesus at the Jordan and here the first conversation with the Risen One.

What may he have said on the road to Emmaus? What did he tell them in the forty days before his Ascension to the Father? It says only that he taught them about the Kingdom of God: "Beginning with Moses and all the prophets, he interpreted to them in all the Scriptures the things concerning himself." We have no tape recording, but we have a tradition that comes from Jesus. No doubt the disciples remembered what he said to them. It left an impression on them, and they told it to others. Even though it was not written down, nevertheless it entered into the life of the Church. Year after year, the Church celebrates the road to Emmaus, where Jesus opens up the Scriptures for us and gives us a glimpse of all that was said about him.

To this day, the Church does what Jesus did on the road to Emmaus, for example at the Easter Vigil. The Easter Vigil, we might say, comes directly from what Jesus explained to the disciples in the days after his Resurrection. If we enter into this great celebration, then it is as though Jesus were accompanying us like the disciples in Emmaus and opening up the Scriptures for us. In the following catechesis, I would like to investigate a bit of the Easter Vigil and see how the meaning of the Resurrection is revealed in it.

The Easter Vigil begins with the light. We come into the dark church, and only the Easter candle is burning. Three times the celebrant sings, "Christ our Light". This light spreads. Then the deacon at the front of the church sings the praise of the Easter candle, the Easter Light, and thereby praises Christ as the Light that shines in the darkness: "The night will be as bright as day, . . . sets [us] apart . . . from the gloom of sin" (Easter Proclamation, *Exsultet*). And then in this light of the Easter candle begins a long liturgy of readings, seven readings from the Old Testament and two from the New Testament. Exactly the same thing happens on this long journey, three readings from the Books of Moses and four from the prophets, as happened with Jesus on the road to Emmaus: he opened up Scripture for them and showed them why the Messiah had to suffer, why there was the Cross, and why at the conclusion stands the Resurrection. To go over the whole Easter Vigil would take a very long time. But I would like to indicate briefly how the Easter Vigil is the continuation of the road to Emmaus and why we then sing Alleluia with so much joy when we encounter the Risen One.

In the Beginning

It begins with three readings from the Books of Moses, the creation account (Gen 1:1–2:2), the sacrifice of Abraham (Gen 22:1–18), and then the passage through the Red Sea (Ex 14:15–15:1). "In the beginning God created the heavens and the earth" (Gen 1:1). Our belief in the Resurrection is not belief in just any miracle, but, first of all, belief in the Creator of heaven and earth, belief in the God who created everything. Gilbert Keith Chesterton (d. 1936) allegedly once said with his pungent wit: "When a man stops believing in God, he doesn't then believe in nothing, he believes in anything." When someone no longer believes in God the Creator, then he believes in anything whatsoever, then he believes in stones and all sorts of esoteric things, in horoscopes, then he believes in fate, then he believes anything at all, instead of believing the one thing, in God the Creator of heaven and earth.

If we believe that Jesus is risen, then we hear the words he spoke before his Ascension on the mountain in Galilee, probably on the Mount of the Beatitudes. These words are mighty, and we can really accept them only in faith. If we think that someone who was only a man said them, then that would be madness! Jesus says:

> All authority in heaven and on earth has been given to me. Go therefore and make disciples of all nations, baptizing them in the name of the Father and of the Son and of the Holy Spirit, teaching them to observe all that I have com-

manded you; and behold, I am with you always, to the close of the age. (Mt 28:18–20)

If we do not believe that God is the Creator of heaven and earth, that *everything* is his creation, that everything is his property, that everything is in his hand, then such words spoken by Jesus are utterly absurd. I quoted these words in my lecture at the Imam Sadiq University, an Islamic university in Teheran, in order to tell the students and professors that both of us, Islam and Christianity, have an absolute faith. I quoted these words of Jesus, which for us Christians are the key words: "All authority in heaven and on earth has been given to me. Go therefore and make disciples of all nations." Those who accompanied me were able to observe this better than I. They said that at that moment a very heavy silence fell over the auditorium. Then I added: "And for you, the Qur'an is the absolute revelation, the will of God that is intended for all men."

This is our faith: Christ is risen from the dead. That is not just any marvel that took place, but he is the Son of God, about whom John says: "All things were made through him, and without him was not anything made that was made" (Jn 1:3). Paul says: "All things were created . . . for him" (Col 1:16), he is truly the center.

Abraham

The next step in the Emmaus catechesis at the Easter Vigil is in stark contrast to the previous one: the story of Abraham. God called Abraham forth and promised him: "I will make of you a great nation . . . and by you all the families of the earth shall bless themselves" (Gen 12:2–3; 13:16;

15:5; 22:17–18). Now God demands of this Abraham that he should give him his only son, on whom the whole promise and all Abraham's hope depend. Saint Paul describes this in the Letter to the Romans as follows:

> He [Abraham] is the father of us all, as it is written, "I have made you the father of many nations"—in the presence of the God in whom he believed, who gives life to the dead and calls into existence the things that do not exist. In hope he believed against hope, that he should become the father of many nations; as he had been told, "So shall your descendants be." He did not weaken in faith when he considered his own body, which was as good as dead because he was about a hundred years old, or when he considered the barrenness of Sarah's womb. No distrust made him waver concerning the promise of God, but he grew strong in his faith as he gave glory to God. (Rom 4:17–20)

This means that Abraham was ready to sacrifice to God his only son, on whom the whole promise depended. "In hope he believed against hope." And right before that Paul mentions "the God in whom he believed", who created everything out of nothing and "gives life to the dead". If we do not believe that God is the Creator, how can we then believe that there is a Resurrection? Abraham believed in *the* God the Creator and trusted that God can make his words come true.

How moving it is, when the lector reads about how Abraham was supposed to sacrifice his son! Abraham goes with his son Isaac to the mountain that God shows him; they begin to climb the mountain: "So they went both of them together. And Isaac said to his father Abraham, 'My father!' And he said, 'Here am I, my son.' He said, 'Behold, the fire and the wood; but where is the lamb for a burnt offering?' Abraham said, 'God will provide himself the lamb for a burnt offering, my son.' So they went both of them together" (Gen 22:6-8). Isaac does not yet know that he is supposed to be the sacrifice: "God will provide himself the lamb. . . ." We can imagine how Jesus on the road to Emmaus explained this passage to his disciples. Since then, they hear this story again and again and remember: "God so loved the world that he gave his only-begotten Son, that whoever believes in him should not perish but have eternal life" (Jn 3:16).

Then God speaks to Abraham: "Because you have done this, and have not withheld your son, your only-begotten, son, I will indeed bless you" (Gen 22:16-17). And again we hear, as Jesus says to his disciples, what Paul then hands on to us: "He who did not spare his own Son but gave him up for us all, will he not also give us all things with him?" (Rom 8:32).

In this second reading at the Easter Vigil, we are led in a moving way to understand why the Messiah had to suffer that, why he is the Lamb of God that the Father sacrificed for us. The Father handed him over for us all, as Paul says: "He . . . became obedient unto death. . . . Therefore God has highly exalted him" (Phil 2:8-9). He died on the Cross, and God reawakened him. Abraham is the just man who withheld nothing from God. In him we see the foreshadowing of Christ, who withheld nothing from the Father. He gave him everything; he was completely obedient to him. Jesus is the Son, through and through. The Little Flower, Saint Thérèse (d. 1897), once said, shortly before her death: "Je n'ai jamais rien refusé à Dieu."—"I never refused God anything." It takes a lot of courage to say something like that, but she was able to say it: "I never refused God anything." How wonderful it is when a person can say that.

That is the basis of our Easter joy, the fact that we can say: He was obedient to the end, to the very last, indeed, even to death on the Cross; he was the true witness, so much so that we can see the Father in him without any distortion whatsoever.

On one occasion, Jesus says, "He who sees me sees [the Father]" (Jn 12:45). There is no gesture, no attitude, no word, no thought of Jesus that distorts God in any way. Jesus is the perfect image of the Father. He never chose himself. As Paul said, "Christ did not please himself" (Rom 15:3). That is why God exalted him, in other words, raised him up; that is why he shines, that is why the light of the Father shines in him. That is the reason for Easter joy. That presupposes, of course, that we bear this certainty in our heart. There is nothing more beautiful and more fortunate than to do the will of the Father. That is real happiness, real humanity. How often, though, we obscure the image of God through our behavior! If we are of the opinion that we become happy only if we concentrate on ourselves as much as possible, fulfill ourselves as much as possible, then we do not understand Easter joy. Easter joy is this: In the Resurrection of Jesus, God confirmed that this man is really his beloved Son. "This is my beloved Son", he says at the baptism in the Jordan (Mt 3:17 and parallel passages). "This is my beloved Son, . . . listen to him", God says at the Transfiguration (Mt 17:5 and parallel passages). He calls to us: In him you can see what I am like and how your path should look. In him you can see what it looks like really to be a man and to become a man!

"Je n'ai jamais rien refusé à Dieu", says Thérèse; "I never refused God anything." That is possible only because Jesus rose from the dead and because he sent his Spirit into our hearts. That is why there are people who can say something like that without lying; that is why we are on this path. Easter joy is also joy over the fact that there are so many disciples of Jesus in whom the obedience of Jesus to the Father is alive, in whom Abraham really acquires descendants: "I will multiply your descendants as the stars of heaven and as the sand which is on the seashore" (Gen 22:17). The descendants of Abraham are those who do the will of the Father, who, like Jesus, with him and through him, accept the Father's will in their lives. Thereby they become a Christ who continues to live; they become Church. Church is nothing other than the Christ who continues to live, his living Body in the world, through whom the Resurrection becomes visible, learnable.

The Red Sea

Surely on the road to Emmaus and in the time after Easter, Jesus revealed to his disciples the meaning of the third reading. They read it during the Last Supper, the story about the departure from Egypt, about the rescue at the Red Sea. The Book of Exodus reports how the people of Israel were saved from a desperate situation. As Egyptian troops were arriving in a constant stream, the sea parted, and they were able to pass through the sea dry-shod. On that occasion, a people was saved. Ever since Jesus arose and gave the command to baptize, "Go therefore and make disciples of all nations, baptizing them" (Mt 28:19), what happened to one people in their rescue through the Red Sea has happened countless times through baptism. So we read in the prayer after the third reading at the Easter Vigil:

> O God, whose ancient wonders remain undimmed in splendor even in our day, for what you once bestowed on a single people, freeing them from Pharaoh's persecution by

the power of your right hand, now you bring about as
the salvation of the nations through the waters of rebirth,
grant, we pray, that the whole world may become children
of Abraham and inherit the dignity of Israel's birthright.
    Through Christ our Lord.

We ought to look now also at the four readings from the
prophets (Is 54:5–14; 55:1–11; Bar 3:9–15, 32–4:4; Ezek
36:16–17a, 18–28), all of which speak about how God led
his people out of slavery, how God establishes a new covenant, how his love is more faithful than all the unfaithfulness
of his people.

One thing that Jesus surely explained to his disciples is
the great reading that we heard on Good Friday and that
the Church has persisted to read since Easter, because it
speaks so clearly about Jesus. We are all familiar with it, the
great reading from the prophet Isaiah (52:13–53:12), where
Jesus showed them that the prophet was speaking about him:
"The righteous one, my servant, [shall] make many to be ac-
counted righteous; and he shall bear their iniquities. Therefore I will divide him a portion with the great, and he shall
divide the spoil with the strong; because he poured out his
soul to death, and was numbered with the transgressors; yet
he bore the sin of many, and made intercession for the transgressors" (Is 53:11–12). "With his stripes we are healed" (Is
53:5).

At the Easter Vigil, when we intone the Gloria and the
Alleluia, then this road of Jesus that he traveled with the
disciples to Emmaus has become our road, too. When the
two disciples return from Emmaus to Jerusalem, they are
greeted by the disciples there: "The Lord has risen indeed,
and has appeared to Simon!" (Lk 24:34). That is the Good
News that greets them in Jerusalem.

What Has Changed?

Of course, we could talk extensively about the fact that the historical reports are reliable. I will mention only three points: First, without the empty tomb in Jerusalem, the news that Jesus is risen could not have lasted a single day. If there were a tomb in Jerusalem in which he was still lying, the disciples could not have spoken about the Resurrection. Second, the appearances were certainly not just images presented to the soul or the imagination but, rather, physical observations. Third, something about the disciples changed. They were fearful no more. They no longer locked themselves in but, rather, appeared in public courageously and had truly become his witnesses. That is perhaps the strongest sign of the Resurrection: They became the community of his witnesses.

What does the Easter faith contribute to our time? Has anything really changed through the Resurrection of Jesus? What does belief in the Resurrection mean for us today? As Christians, we must reflect through the message of the Resurrection that we become Church again in the sense in which the disciples became Church then. The Risen One gathered them together; they put aside their fear and their anxiety, but also their self-centeredness. Then and now, the Lord reproves unbelief and reawakens faith.

I would like to conclude with a passage by a theologian that greatly impressed me. Gerhard Lohfink wrote a book that has the beautiful title *Gottes Volksbegehren*: God's desire for a people. Gerhard Lohfink asks the question: Where does disbelief come from today with regard to the Resurrection?

There are many reasons for it. One of these reasons is surely the deep-seated inferiority complex of Christians, who since the Enlightenment (two hundred years ago) have had drummed into them incessantly the idea that Christianity did not change the world. . . .

Christianity supposedly did not change the world for the better? The fact that the Sermon on the Mount was formulated supposedly did not change the world? The early Christian communities that refused to adore the Roman Caesar as God, and through their refusal unmasked the arrogance of every state that acts as if it were God, supposedly did not change the world? The many Christian martyrs from the first century to this day, who preferred to die rather than to give up the truth of their faith and who in this way showed that the truth is stronger than power, supposedly did not change the world? All the saints who lived unknown among us down to Francis of Assisi or Teresa of Avila supposedly did not change the world with their joy in doing the will of God? All the monasteries and convents that covered Austria since the early Middle Ages like stars in the sky—with their schools, their pharmacies, their workshops, their scriptoria [writing rooms], with their architecture and their agriculture—they supposedly did not change the world? All the mothers who sat at their children's bedside night after night and recited an evening prayer with them and looked at the preceding day once again with the eyes of faith supposedly did not change the world? All the married couples who did not give in to the trends of the times, did not get divorced but, rather, remained together faithfully and were reconciled with one another again and again, supposedly did not change the world? All the religious women who kept night watch at the bedside of the dying, washed the seriously ill, and consoled the sorrowful supposedly did not change the world? . . . We have no idea what the world would

look like today if the Christian faith were not there. . . .
If he had not risen, the world would be lost. I am convinced that
in this sentence [from the German Easter hymn] there is
more truth than we realize. If Jesus had not risen from the
dead and if his Resurrection had not started a quiet but un-
relenting revolution, the world would look different today,
indeed, it would perhaps have long since been destroyed.[1]

[1] Gerhard Lohfink, *Gottes Volksbegehren: Biblische Herausforderungen* (Munich: Verlag Neue Stadt, 1998), 83–85.

VIII

"Holy Mary, Pray for Us"
On the Meaning of Marian Devotion

Regina coeli, laetare, alleluia;
Quia quem meruisti portare, alleluia;
Resurrexit sicut dixit, alleluia;
Ora pro nobis Deum, alleluia.

O Queen of heaven, rejoice, alleluia;
For he whom thou didst merit to bear, alleluia;
Is risen as he said, alleluia;
Pray for us to God, alleluia.

Experiences of Mary's Intercession

On May 13, 1981, at 5:19 P.M. on Saint Peter's Square, a gun was shot at Pope John Paul II. The nine-millimeter bullet had been fired by Ali Agca, who was an excellent shot. He was pardoned on June 13, 2000, by the Italian President, to the joy of the pope, who had been requesting it for a long time. The bullet hit the pope in his abdomen and is said to have caused massive internal bleeding in a short time. The surgeons at the Gemelli Clinic, who operated for hours on the pope and battled for his life, which was hanging by a slender thread, determined that the bullet had missed the main artery [and his spinal column] by a few millimeters and thus had hit none of the vital nerve centers. As the pope later put it: "One hand fired, and another guided the bullet."

It was May 13, the day of the first Fatima appearance. The pope himself said that he was not yet aware then of the full significance of Fatima. But as soon as he could, he had the source materials about the events in Fatima brought to him in the Gemelli Clinic, including the text of the so-called "third secret", which he read and then sent back to the archive, where it remained in safekeeping until May 13, 2000. On that day, the pope through his Secretary of State unexpectedly announced in Fatima what the essential contents of this third secret are. Shortly thereafter, the exact text was published with an explanatory commentary by Cardinal Joseph Ratzinger.

Since May 13, 1981, the pope's reverence and love for Our Lady of Fatima has been unmistakable. I will recall only three dates. 1. Exactly one year after the assassination attempt, in 1982, he made a pilgrimage of thanksgiving to Fatima. 2. In 1984, as a spontaneous gesture, he handed the bishop of Fatima a little jewel case containing the bullet that had hit him. This bullet was set in the crown of the statue of Our Lady of Fatima. 3. Finally another gesture: in the Holy Year, on May 13, 2000, when he visited Fatima again, the pope presented the episcopal ring that Cardinal Wyszynski had given him when he became pope, on which his motto, *Totus tuus*, is engraved, to Our Lady of Fatima as a gift.

This catechesis is about "experiences of Mary's intercession". By this I mean experiences that are quite concrete, are by no means isolated instances, and occur in a great variety of ways throughout the long history of Christianity. These are experiences of Mary's help. In Vienna, there is a street, Marienhilfstrasse, that is so called because there is a church of Our Lady of Perpetual Help on it. Because for centuries people have had the experience that Mary shows herself to be a mother, a helper in all needs, such churches can be found in many localities.

I will come back again to May 13, 1981. On that day the pope signed the founding document for an institute that was especially dear to his heart and is so to this day [2001]. It bears his name: John Paul II Institute for Studies on Marriage and Family. The family is a major theme in his pontificate. He has often repeated the statement, "The future of humanity passes by way of the family."

On that same day, May 13, 1981, the pope also signed another founding document. He founded the Pontifical Academy for Life, an academy whose scientific, medical, biological, legal, and theological task is to study questions that have to do with life. He appointed the famous French researcher Jérôme Lejeune as the first president of this academy. Jérôme Lejeune was his guest at lunch on that May 13. He was a great defender of life, especially of handicapped life, and discovered the cause of Down syndrome, or trisomy 21, the genetic defect that used to be called mongolism. Until Lejeune's death from cancer, the pope maintained a cordial friendship with him.

Also on that May 13, 1981, a big demonstration for the legalization of abortion organized by the Communist Party was to take place in Rome in the evening. When news spread of the assassination attempt on the pope, the organizers called off the demonstration. This shows in a peculiar way how a culture of life and a culture of death are interwoven and in conflict with each other on a given day.

Let us try to investigate such experiences of Mary's intercession more deeply. What is the status of Marian devotion? What is the reason for honoring Mary? Certainly it is these experiences, which obviously occur in all generations. But what is the justification for Marian devotion, and where are its limits? How do we distinguish erroneous forms of Marian devotion from correct, "sound" forms of Marian devotion?

When the pope was struck by the bullet and collapsed, he is said to have murmured in Polish, his mother tongue, "Mary, my Mother, my Mother!" *Totus tuus*, the motto on the pope's coat of arms, testifies that his special intimacy with Mary did not begin on May 13, 1981. But from then on, the theme of gratitude became even stronger, and again and again there are reminders of his profound gratitude for the help that he received. But obviously Marian devotion already played a role much earlier in the pope's life. He lost his mother when he was nine and his only brother when he was twelve years old. His father died when Karol Wojtyła was twenty. He himself says that Mary became his mother early on. The Marian devotion of his Polish people no doubt played a major role. But in his case, it also has a very personal note, a deep impression left by the great pilgrimages to Jasna Góra in Częstochowa, as he himself said there: "How often I have said here *Totus tuus*, I am all yours." The life of the pope speaks eloquently of this profound gratitude and a strong, unsentimental trust in Mary. I had the privilege of being present on October 8, 2000: at the climax of the bishops' pilgrimage for the Holy Year, he recited before the statue of Our Lady of Fatima a long prayer that he called the "Affidamento" of the third millennium to Mary, the entrusting of the new millennium to Mary.

Mary, Mother of God

Many other examples could be mentioned, instances of Mary's help that we ourselves have experienced, that we have heard about, that are documented in history and in the present. But once again the question: Why? Why this special veneration of Mary? I would like to begin with the question that is surely the most difficult and most important, when we hear objections against Marian devotion, but also when it is a matter of discerning: What is wrong, and what is along the right lines, along the lines of the Gospel?

Is venerating Mary not in opposition to adoring Christ and worshipping God? Does Marian devotion not often act as a filter or a screen in front of the true worship of God and Christ that is commanded by faith? The Catechism says quite soberly: "What the Catholic faith believes about Mary is based on what it believes about Christ." But it adds: "What it teaches about Mary illumines in turn its faith in Christ" (CCC 487). What we believe about Mary is based on our faith in Christ but also makes it clearer. Mary's role results entirely from Christ's role. But it also makes Christ's role clearer to us. Everything depends on how we see Christ. If Jesus is a special man, a prophet, then Mary is the mother of a special man. There are many mothers of many special men in the history of mankind. That would not justify attributing a special significance to her. But if he is the Messiah of Israel, the Son of God, then she is really "the Mother of God" in the sense in which the Church understands this: she is the mother of the Son of God made man. But then Marian devotion is inseparable from devotion to Christ. This is precisely where the criticism begins. At this flash point, there is a lot of uneasiness about the Marian devotion of Catholics and also of the Eastern Orthodox. Is she not secretly being exalted as a goddess on a throne, on the altar, and somehow being equated with Christ, indeed, made equal to God?

In an Islamic country, if one hears or reads the expression "Mother of God", one is frightened, because for Muslims that is probably one of the most blasphemous expressions imaginable. How can anyone say that a human being is God's mother? Has a deification of Mary not taken place here? These are old accusations that are made over and over again. Marian devotion is thought to be basically the worship of the great mother gods of the ancient religions, taken up again and, so to speak, "baptized". Isis and Osiris are repeatedly depicted in the Egyptian religions, the goddess with the child, and that is the model for Mary with the Child, they are fond of saying. Likewise the great Artemis of Ephesus, the goddess of fertility. Paul had several conflicts with the silversmiths of Ephesus, because with his critique of idols he endangered their business. This led to the dramatic riot of the silversmiths of Ephesus (Acts 19:21–40), who were incited to gather in the stadium in Ephesus and shout, "Great is Artemis of the Ephesians!" (Acts 19:28). When we see, then, that precisely there in Ephesus in the year 431, not quite four hundred years later, the Council declared Mary the Mother of God, does that not arouse the suspicion that this designation of Mary as the Mother of God was just the baptism of the pagan mother goddesses? Were not many of our ancient Marian shrines originally places of pagan worship, which in this way were "Christianized"? This view is intriguing at first, and it is often presented with conviction: Was it not basically a clever policy of Christianity simply to "Christianize" the gods by "covering them over" with saints?

In terms of purely external appearances, that undoubtedly seems self-evident. But when you look more closely and ask, "Why was that possible? Why could they build Marian shrines, of all things, or other shrines on the sites of old pagan places of worship?" then more in-depth questions become necessary. Yes, there must have been experiences of salvation here, experiences of Mary's help. I am thinking, for example, of the Marian shrine in Kleinmariazell in Lower Austria. Probably it was a pagan place of worship. But on this spot two feuding brothers experienced reconciliation. There, over this spring and shrine, they extended to each other a handshake of reconciliation. Was that not an experience of salvation that led to Mary being honored there as a helper? At least this way of viewing things would have to be taken into account when discussing the "Christianization" of pagan models or precursors.

Mary and the One Mediator

What is the faith background for the experience of Mary's closeness? Obviously what causes offense again and again is the designation of Mary as Mediatrix, Auxiliatrix, as someone who distributes graces, as someone who mediates salvation. Does that not belong to Christ alone? Does Paul not say: He is the "one mediator between God and men" (1 Tim 2:5)? Has something foreign not intruded here that actually has no place in our Christian faith? The more comprehensive question is: Did Mary really cooperate in our salvation? Did the saints cooperate in our salvation? Can we cooperate in the salvation of others? Or does God accomplish his work all alone, as it were, and when there are instruments, then only quite passive ones who do not cooperate of themselves but are, so to speak, only channels? Was Mary a passive instrument, or is there something like an active cooperation of Mary in salvation, so that we can correctly say that we experience help from her?

There are two convictions behind this belief that Mary is a helper and a mediatrix, which is taken for granted and lived out in the Church: First, we, who are creatures of God, can really cooperate in God's work. Second, Mary did this in a unique and incomparably excellent way. A rather difficult passage from the Second Vatican Council expresses this. Chapter 8 of the Dogmatic Constitution on the Church, *Lumen gentium*, deals with Mary in God's plan of salvation and her place in the Church. This dense passage takes up the question: Can we really call Mary a Mediatrix? In it we read:

> There is but one Mediator as we know from the words of the apostle, "for there is but one God and one mediator of God and men, the man Christ Jesus, who gave himself [as] a redemption for all" (1 Tim 2:5–6). The maternal duty of Mary toward men in no wise obscures or diminishes this unique mediation of Christ, but rather shows His power. For all the salvific influence of the Blessed Virgin on men originates, not from some inner necessity, but from the divine pleasure. It flows forth from the superabundance of the merits of Christ, rests on His mediation, depends entirely on it and draws all its power from it. In no way does it impede, but rather does it foster the immediate union of the faithful with Christ.[1]

Mary is not a screen or a shield that covers Christ; rather, she shows forth Christ's power and thereby fosters our union with him. The coat of arms of Pope John Paul II has a cross with the letter M under it, the sign of Mary, and under that the motto *Totus tuus*. Is complete dedication of oneself to Mary not an obstacle with regard to Christ? The pope has shown again and again that that is precisely not the case.

Lumen gentium goes on to say that Mary "is invoked by the Church under the titles of Advocate, Auxiliatrix, Adjutrix, and Mediatrix". There are quite a few people who think that it is time for the Church to proclaim as a dogma that Mary is the Mediatrix of All Graces. Again and again

[1] *Lumen gentium* 60.

the pope is asked to do this. I set this question completely aside here. But the Council does in fact say that she is called "Mediatrix". And it also adds: "This, however, is to be so understood that it neither takes away from nor adds anything to the dignity and efficaciousness of Christ the one Mediator."[2]

An important clarification follows: "No creature could ever be counted as equal with the Incarnate Word and Redeemer", not even Mary; not even she stands on the same level as Christ. She simply cannot be classified as his equal. To explain this, the Council gives two examples.

1. "Just as the priesthood of Christ is shared in various ways both by the ministers and by the faithful",[3] so it is also with Mary in relation to Christ. We believe that there is actually only one priest. The Letter to the Hebrews says this quite explicitly: There is *only one priest in the New Covenant*, Jesus Christ (cf. Heb 8:1). Why then are some men called priests, or even bishops and cardinals? Why are all baptized persons called priests, according to the universal priesthood of all the baptized? The Council says that there is a sharing in the one priesthood of Christ.[4] We profess that there is really only one Mediator between God and men but that we may cooperate because Christ has called us to do so.

2. "The one goodness of God is really communicated in different ways to His creatures."[5] When the rich young man comes to Jesus and says, "Good Teacher, what must I do to inherit eternal life?" Jesus answers him rather brusquely: "Why do you call me good? No one is good but God alone"

---

[2] Ibid., 62.
[3] Ibid.
[4] Ibid., 10.
[5] Ibid., 62.

(Mk 10:17–18). We profess that God alone can really be called good. Nevertheless, the Council says, there is a participation in the goodness of God in his creatures. A good beer on a hot summer day is really something good. It takes part in the goodness of the Creator. Goodness really does exist, as the Council says so beautifully, poured out on creatures. When we do a good deed, then that is not competition with God; rather, we are privileged to participate in the one who alone is good.

That may sound very theoretical at first. But it makes a central point of our faith. We believe that man is God's image, a likeness of the living God. God is unique, incomparable, and nevertheless there are images of God. We are God's image and likeness, says the Book of Genesis (Gen 1:26). It also means, though, that we participate in God's activity, that we can cooperate in his work. This is true of every human being. Even the most miserable person is still to be respected in his incomparable dignity as an image of God. That is why we are convinced that every person, even one convicted of a serious crime, should be spared and that his life is sacred. That is why, as I believe, the death penalty is ultimately and essentially not in keeping with the fact that man is the image of God. Yet there are people about whom we can say in a special way that they make God's image visible, so to speak. We call them the saints. When we say that man is the image of God, then we are also saying that a responsibility is connected with it. The biblical expression "image of God" can also be translated: "vizier of God", "administrator", "someone delegated by God". We have the responsibility to collaborate in God's work.

This leads to a criterion that is applicable to Marian devotion, also. The cult of the saints must always prove itself in an imitation of the saints, too. It is not enough just to venerate the saints; we must also strive to be like them. That means quite specifically to imitate the responsibility that they took. The question of imitating the saints is always the measure for authentic veneration of the saints in the Church, too. The criterion for the authenticity of holiness is whether someone lived out his responsibility as an image of God. That is why authentic Marian devotion always involves this, also, and includes a willingness to accept responsibility.

It is not up to us to judge whether the pope's devotion to Mary is authentic. But we can say one thing with certainty: his veneration of Mary does not lead him away from people. It does not lead him into a cranky ghetto; rather, it strengthens his unmistakable responsibility for people. Devotion to Mary always means also in a special way the willingness to imitate Mary's self-giving, to follow her example. When Mary says to Jesus at the wedding feast in Cana, "They have no wine" (Jn 2:3), this shows her attentiveness to the needs and troubles of other people. So another criterion for the authenticity of Marian devotion must be the willingness to imitate Mary's attentiveness to the needs of others.

Marian devotion, which should always be imitation as well, does not lead away from Christ or away from other people; rather, it brings us closer to Christ and closer to others.

Mary, Mother of Mankind

I would like to broach another question: Why, then, does Mary have a special place? Why is she especially prominent among all the saints we venerate? The answer is simple and sheds the light of faith on the matter. I would like to address the question in terms of an experience that is probably familiar to all of us. There are situations in which we realize: Now it is up to me! This is a situation in which I cannot make any excuses or let someone else deal with it. If I seize the opportunity, then good; if I miss the chance, then it is lost, not only for me but also for others. There are situations in which I and I alone am required.

The tower of Saint Stephen's Cathedral in Vienna is standing because in 1945 one man, Captain Klinkicht, recognized a moment like that and seized it. He was the commander of the air defense of Vienna; he received the order to shoot down the tower of Saint Stephen's and refused to carry out that order—at the risk of being shot himself—and he transmitted the rejection of this order to all the anti-aircraft artillery turrets in Vienna. There are moments when things depend utterly and entirely on my response, "Yes, now!" If I miss the moment, it is lost.

In the history of mankind there was one moment when, so to speak, everything was at stake, everything was placed in one hand. That was the hour of the Annunciation. If we contemplate that hour when the angel brought to Mary the message, "You will conceive in your womb and bear a son, and you shall call his name Jesus" (Lk 1:31), in that hour everything really was in her hands and depended on her cooperation, on her Yes or No.

There are such hours in our own lives, also. Often I wonder: What is it like in vocation stories when someone hears the call to follow? There is also the situation of the rich young man, who at that hour, at that moment, goes away sorrowful (Mk 10:17–31). I trust that God did not reject the rich young man. Yet his No brought Jesus to tears, as did the No of his people, who would not consent (cf. Mt 23:37).

Mary, however, said Yes in the decisive hour, and in that hour she became the woman who brought salvation for us all. Not that she brought about salvation; salvation comes from God. But she said Yes. I picture it this way: so much, such a wealth lies in this Yes of Mary, in that one hour, that all generations can draw from it, because that hour had such importance. To return once again to Saint Stephen's Cathedral, naturally we do not think about Captain Klinkicht every time we see the tower. But if he had not said No to that order then, in the decisive hour, then we would not see the tower today.

Of course, Mary then lived out this Yes in the everyday routine of faith, in the many hours, days, and years in which she walked along that path. Saint Irenaeus, an early Christian writer from the second century, says somewhere: "In her obedience she became the cause of salvation for the whole human race." Not that she *wrought* salvation; rather she *obtained* it for us. Not that she is the first cause of salvation, but she is indeed an accessory cause, through whom God was able to do his work. Through this Yes, she became the salutary woman for all times. Since then, this abundance that comes from her Yes overflows onto all generations. When in Lourdes or in Fatima you see the countless people who come and place their trust in her, then you sense what power lies in this one decisive hour.

In that hour in which she said Yes, she became not only the Mother of the Redeemer, but also the Mother of all for whom he is Redeemer. She is called the Mother of mankind, because he is the Redeemer for all mankind. That is probably the most profound reason why people in all nations and in all ages have such trust in her.

IX

Hope That Reaches beyond Death

Longing for Eternal Life

Hope that reaches beyond death is the topic of our final catechesis. I would like to begin with a passage from the *Confessions* of Saint Augustine (d. 430), with an excerpt from
book 9. Augustine has come to believe. After a long strug-
gle he has been baptized by Ambrose (d. 397) in Milan and
now is with his mother, Monica, on the return trip to his
hometown in North Africa. In Ostia they make a stopover.
Augustine recounts:

> When the day on which she [Monica] was to depart this
> life was near at hand (Thou knewest the day[, O God];
> we did not), I believe it happened by Thy management,
> in Thy hidden ways, that she and I were standing alone,
> leaning on a window from which the garden inside the
> house we occupied could be viewed. It was at Ostia on
> the Tiber, where, far removed from the crowds after the
> hardship of a long journey, we were resting in preparation
> for the sea voyage.
>
> We were talking to each other alone, very sweetly, "for-
> getting what is behind, straining forward to what is be-
> fore" (Phil 3:13). Between us, "in the present truth" (2 Pet
> 1:12), which Thou art, we tried to find out what the eter-
> nal life of the saints would be, which "eye has not seen nor
> ear heard, nor hast it entered into the heart of man" (1 Cor
> 2:9). But, we also yearned with the mouth of our heart for
> the supernal flood from "Thy Fountain, the Fountain of

Life which is with Thee" (Ps 36:9), so that, having been sprinkled from it as much as our capacity would permit, we might think in some way about such a great thing.

. . . [O]ur talk had reached the conclusion that the greatest delight of the bodily senses, in the brightest bodily light, was not capable of comparison with the joy of that life and, moreover, did not seem worthy of being mentioned.[1]

Somewhat farther on in this conversation about eternal life, Augustine says that they "did touch . . . a little, with an all-out thrust of [their] hearts", the reality for which they were yearning, eternal life.[2] Shortly thereafter, Monica died in Ostia. Augustine buried her and then traveled on to North Africa.

With Augustine and Monica, we are on the lookout for eternal life. Do we have, as they did, a longing for heaven, for eternal life, a yearning to come home and to be at home there? May I joyfully look forward to eternal life? May I yearn for it? Or is that fleeing from the world, shirking responsibility? Can I look forward to eternal life? Should I not much rather be afraid when I think about the hour of reckoning? When I reflect that I must give an account for my life: What will that hour look like? On which side will I get to stand? Did the Lord not clearly say that there will be a division: those on the right hand and those on the left, the former marked out for life and the others for corruption (Mt 25:31–46)? And so, on the one hand, the question: May I long with my whole heart and reach out for eternal life? On the other hand, the question: Can I miss the goal of my life? Can I be lost forever?

[1] Augustine, *Confessions* IX, 10, 23–24, trans. by Vernon J. Bourke (New York: Fathers of the Church, 1953), 250–51.

[2] Ibid., 252.

We are confronted here with an obscure mystery. But since the Enlightenment there has been a suspicion that the obscurity of this mystery is actually clerical fear-mongering, a threat of hell, in order to scare people so that they will be well-behaved and decent. Nowadays, in contrast, it appears that we are all going to heaven because a banal existential outlook has trained us to say that "we are good." At the same time, many people have the sense that that simply will not work without justice. It cannot be such a simple matter that good and evil have no consequences at all, that in the final outcome it makes no difference how I live and what I do. Would that not make everything arbitrary? Does justice not lose its exquisite character as well as its seriousness if justice and injustice are ultimately treated alike before the judgment seat of God?

Another variation on the theme, which is very widespread today, abandons the very idea that it is up to God to pass judgment. Instead, it expects a sort of "never-ending self-judgment" in the form of reincarnation. These rebirths exist so that, in the many lives that we have already lived or will yet live, we can reduce the *karma* that we have accumulated, the consequences of what is evil and harmful in our life. Many see in this a sort of justice. They claim that I myself would have the chance in a future life to make good whatever I have messed up in this life.

Faith tells us in no uncertain terms that there is only this one earthly life. I would rather not outline here the debate over whether there are passages in Sacred Scripture that may speak about some sort of reincarnation, about future, additional lives on this earth. I think I can say that no passage from Scripture can sensibly be interpreted as proof of the doctrine of reincarnation. Our faith tells us that there is only this one life and, afterward—eternal life. That means, however, that every moment of this life is unique, irreplaceable. What is past is gone, unrepeatable, and therefore so precious, too. Ultimately, that is probably also the reason why time is valuable to us: because it cannot be repeated arbitrarily.

Our faith also teaches, of course, that there is the possibility of purification, that at death our earthly journey is indeed definitively over but that we can intercede for one another so that purification might take place after death. Otherwise, praying for the dead would be meaningless. The Church's practice throughout the centuries shows that prayer for the dead can help them. The many epitaphs in the cathedral remind us of this faith, and so does everything involved in our funeral rites.

Questions about the End

We mean the questions about heaven, hell, and purgatory. These are the topics connected with the end of human life, which in theology are called the "Last Things". How often do we hear sermons about them? I can remember in my childhood. Our pastor, who was already up in years, used to preach for a long time, at least I felt that he did. But when he spoke from the pulpit about eternal life, then you knew the sermon was coming to an end. For at the conclusion, there was always talk about eternal life.

Today, you seldom hear about it. This is due, perhaps, to a suspicion that Marxism popularized and that has its effects to this day. It is the suspicion that looking forward to eternal life too intensely could be a consolation prize. Karl Marx accused Christianity, indeed, religion in general, of being opium that makes people forget pain and suffering and promises them a better life in the hereafter. Instead of improving the world, one offers hope for the next world. Marxism has surely played a role in the neglect of the Last Things. I think, though, that today something else is important, too, which to me seems to be even more radical. Often today "wellness" is considered the highest precept in life. More important than right or wrong, than good or evil, is the feeling of well-being. Of course it is very nice when we feel well. But if "wellness" becomes a precept by which I live, then everything is judged by what it obtains for me *now*.

A hymn I often quote has become somehow foreign to our feelings about life: "On earth we are sojourners, / And restlessly we roam / With many sorts of burdens / Toward our heavenly home."[3] Does this line, "On earth we are sojourners", still have any meaning in the basic sense of Christian life today? Is the theme of the brevity of life a theme that motivates us? For centuries it was a long-running theme in the spiritual literature, not only among Christians, but also in antiquity, in Marcus Aurelius, for example. We are only pilgrims; only a short time has been allotted to us. Another part of this sense of the brevity of life is the image of the valley of tears. We live our lives "in hac lacrimarum valle", "in this valley of tears", as it says in the Marian antiphon *Salve Regina*. There are many experiences behind this that today, however, are often not expressed but repressed, instead. And yet, how many things can be borne more easily in this short pilgrimage of our earthly life when we know that we are only sojourners on earth and that this life is spent in a valley of tears. There is something hopeful about the valley of tears image. A valley is not a self-contained basin but has a direction: it leads to an open space in the distance.

[3] Hymn 656 in the *Gotteslob* hymnal.

A valley is not a lead chamber that shuts out what is above but, rather, is open to the sky and to what is ahead, just like our life.

Something that we have come to forget even more, perhaps, is the fact that eternal life already begins now, that in a certain sense we can already find our way home now. The prerequisite, of course, is that we repent, as Jesus says in his first public statement: "Repent, and believe in the gospel" (Mk 1:15). Wherever repentance and conversion take place, new life is experienced. Through Christ, it becomes possible even now to experience eternal life. That is generally, perhaps, the most misunderstood side of the Christian message. There is only one way to life, to a life that no death can destroy, and that is conversion. "Unless you repent you will all likewise perish", says Jesus to those who listen to him in Jerusalem (Lk 13:3-5). But if you repent, then this life, eternal life, can begin even now. Without repentance, nothing works. This is the core of the Christian message.

The Path of Life — The Path of Death

The key words of this catechesis are frightening but—as hopefully we will see—also gladdening. They are the last words of Jesus in the Gospel of Mark. There the Lord says to his disciples: "He who believes and is baptized will be saved; but he who does not believe will be condemned" (Mk 16:16). We see that the "Good News" [Frohbotschaft] and the Bad News [Drohbotschaft] cannot be pitted against each other. It is amazing, and frightening, too, but it is a necessary saying. Our Lord's first words in the Gospel of Mark are: "The kingdom of God is at hand; repent, and believe in the gospel" (Mk 1:15). That is the decisive thing

about the Christian message: the call to make a decision
and to convert. But at the same time, this call contains the
promise: Choose life! Decide on the path of life and not on
the path of death. Already in the Old Testament, it is clearly
set before our eyes: there are two ways; the one leads to
life, and the other leads to death. I must make my decision.
How I decide has its consequences for this life and also for
the next.

If I do not make my decision, then I have already decided
on the path of death. If I make my decision, then I can decide
rightly or wrongly, to strive for the goal or to go astray. If I
have set out on the wrong way, then, thank God, I can often
make a course correction, repent, and seek the right way.
Sometimes I can no longer do that, because the choice of a
path, a wrong path, has consequences that are irreversible.
These consequences hold me and others fast. I have to endure these consequences. But as long as I am on the way, as
long as my earthly journey continues, I can at least be sorry
that I set out on a wrong way. If I am sorry for it, then actually I go back to the place where I chose the wrong way
and acknowledge that that was a wrong choice at that time.
Even though the consequences can no longer be undone,
I can still find a new beginning spiritually by being sorry,
by acknowledging the wrong decision, by being sorry for it
and beginning with a new way. This sorrow is really a new
beginning, even though I must endure the consequences of
my wrong decisions. Jesus is the physician. He gives us the
necessary medicine and makes a new beginning possible.

According to the faith of the Church, the pilgrimage ends
with death. With that, the path I have chosen is definitive.
I have arrived at the goal, and there is no more going back.
Then it is in fact true: either I have missed the way or else
I have found it. That sounds terrible, and it is, too. Then

there can in fact be eternal happiness or eternal unhappiness. Those elements of Jesus' message that speak about this reality have been almost completely filtered out of our sense of Christian life today. The message of Sacred Scripture, however, is clear. I will mention three familiar parables. They are all in a chapter in Matthew's Gospel (chapter 25). Jesus tells these parables in Jerusalem shortly before his Passion in the seriousness of this situation that calls for a decision:

1. The parable of the ten virgins (Mt 25:1–13); five are wise and five foolish. The foolish virgins have brought lamps with them but no oil, and they have to go back again to fetch oil. But when they return, the door is shut, and they have to admit that it is too late. The bridegroom says to them: "Truly, I say to you, I do not know you" (Mt 25:12). With that, Jesus is saying, therefore: There is such a thing as *too late*. There is such a thing as missing the opportunities. There is such a thing as neglecting to prepare for this hour. Jesus concludes the parable with the saying: "Watch therefore, for you know neither the day nor the hour" (Mt 25:13).

2. The second parable is about the money entrusted to the servants (Mt 25:14–30). A landowner is setting out on a journey. To one of his servants he entrusts five silver talents, to another—two, and to a third—one. The servant who received five and the one who received two traded wisely with their money. To them the landowner in the parable says: "Enter into the joy of your master" (Mt 25:21, 23). About the man who buried his one talent he says: "Cast the worthless servant into the outer darkness, where there will be weeping and gnashing of teeth" (Mt 25:30). Here, too, the parable addresses a situation of making a decision that leads to a definitive, final situation.

3. The best-known parable is the one about the Last Judg-

ment (Mt 25:31−46). The judge will separate the people to the right and to the left. To those on the right he says: "As you did it to one of the least of these my brethren, you did it to me" (Mt 25:40); to those on the left: "As you did it not to one of the least of these, you did it not to me." Then the last verse says: "And they will go away into eternal punishment, but the righteous into eternal life" (Mt 25:45−46).

A child in kindergarten told the parable this way: "To those on the right he says, 'Come, O blessed of my father!' and to those on the left he said, 'Go away, you're getting on my nerves!'" Hear what the mother said to the child at home?!

Longing for a Happy Death

We started with Monica and Augustine in Ostia and their longing for heaven and now have arrived at the "Bad News". But where has the Good News gone? Let us try to bring a little light into this darkness. Two questions confront us here. First: What is eternal life in the first place? Second, the question about the Judgment, about heaven and hell.

Is there such a thing as a continuation of the soul's life after death? The philosophers speculated a lot about this, and there is something like a philosophical proof for the immortality of the soul. And yet this is not primarily a philosophical question. It is, rather, a question about faith and about life. The last article in the Apostles' Creed is: "I believe in . . . life everlasting." I remember how deeply disturbed I was when for the first time, at the age of around sixteen, I encountered in a long evening conversation an adult who was a declared atheist. "You die, and it is all over." It was puzzling to me how anyone could live and think that way. I have since met individuals who think the same way and are wonderful people. I am thinking of one married couple: both of them were extremely committed to helping other people and were very clear about their conviction: With death, everything is over. That makes you very cautious about saying that atheists are simply egotists. Where does someone who does not believe in a life after death get the motivation to live a good life so unselfishly, anyway? There is an even more relevant phenomenon today that disturbs me more deeply than the atheist: eternal life is of no interest at all, because this-worldly things occupy people's attention entirely. There is no room for a question about life after death. Many have lost sight of the hereafter.

Nowhere does this become so clear as in the way we deal with dying. Formerly, the first concern was about dying: How can I get *safely to the hereafter*? How can I help others to make that passage safely? The sodalities "for a happy death" that were found in many localities had precisely this concern: How can I prepare myself well for the hour of death? Am I ready to come before the face of God? Is my life such that it will withstand God's presence? Consequently the concern was mainly with the *transitus*, the passage to the beyond. People recited prayers for the dying.

To a great extent, we have lost sight of one prayer that many people used to know by heart, the so-called *Commendatio animae*, the commending of the soul to its journey home. In Christian tradition, this prayer used to be prayed not only with the priest but also in the family when someone was approaching death. It begins with the words: "Proficiscere anima christiana", literally: "Set out, O Christian soul."

Go forth, Christian soul, from this world
in the name of God the almighty Father,
who created you,

in the name of Jesus Christ, the Son of the living God,
who suffered for you,
in the name of the Holy Spirit,
who was poured out upon you.
Go forth, faithful Christian.

May you live in peace this day,
may your home be with God in Zion,
with Mary, the virgin Mother of God,
with Joseph, and all the angels and saints. . . .

May you return to [your Creator] who formed you from
    the dust of the earth.
May holy Mary, the angels, and all the saints
come to meet you as you go forth from this life. . . .

May you see your Redeemer face to face. (CCC 1020)

How our concern about the dying person has shifted! (This
is not meant as a judgment but only as an observation.)
Nowadays, a good death is thought to be a sudden death
that is quick and painless. For centuries Christians prayed:
"Preserve us from an unforeseen death!" Sudden death was
viewed as an evil, because one might not be prepared. To
be torn suddenly from this life while unprepared and to be
thrust into the finality of eternal life was considered a misfortune.

The effort that is being made in the hospice movement to
care for the dying is magnificent, and it is a clear alternative
to active euthanasia, as it is already practiced in many places.
Yet there is a question that goes farther: Is our sympathy
today not directed above all toward comfort in dying? As
important and right as that may be, is there not a danger
even here that, through our concern about freedom from
pain, we might lose sight of a well-prepared departure and

of the fact that the decisive thing about the hour of death
is that we arrive in the "next world"? If we reflect on this,
we become more aware of the extent to which the gospel
is a *contradiction of the spirit of the age* or, better yet, a *wake-up
call* demonstrating how much Jesus wants to snatch us from
the sleep of indifference or even of self-deception.

I remember a little story in the Gospel of Luke. A rich
man brought in a great harvest. He reflects: "What shall I
do?", tears down his barn, and builds a much larger one.
Then he says to himself: "You have ample goods laid up for
many years; take your ease, eat, drink, be merry." Then God
says to him, "Fool! This night your soul is required of you"
(Lk 12:16-21). Of all that, what will you take with you?
Later Jesus says: Therefore pay attention to what makes you
rich in God's sight (cf. Lk 12:33). That is the revaluation of
all values that Christ brought into our world. Out of this
evangelical revaluation a whole culture arose, a culture of
life and a culture of death. Many of our churches would not
exist without this culture of life and death formed by the
gospel. Everything that archaeologists have found in their
excavations in and around Christian churches, the many
burial places in every century, point toward this culture, in
which there is great knowledge about the significance of the
passage into eternal life. Our churches and cemeteries are
full of testimonies to this concern about a good departure,
about bridges, about a good accompaniment from this life
into the next.

God Wants to Save Us

Let us examine a critical objection. Was all that perhaps
so important to Christians in the past because the clergy
"heated up hell" for them, because people were made to

fear hell? Could there be something positive in the fact that today this fear, as it seems to me, is simply no longer prevalent? Was that fear of hell not really a bad business? Maybe in our time we have seen even more clearly that the warning about the loss of salvation is part of Jesus' message but that this is not the center of his message. Eternal damnation can be found in Jesus' discourses, but it is not central.

I was very surprised when I consulted the concordance to the writings of Saint Thérèse, the Little Flower, in other words, the dictionary with all the terms and all the passages where they occur. I looked under the heading *enfance*, childhood, and it continued for several pages. Then I came upon the word *enfer*, hell. I was surprised that it occurs very infrequently in Thérèse's writings. Has hell diminished in importance not only among the theologians but perhaps even among the saints? Is it possible that a turning point has arrived that was defined and approved, so to speak, from above, by heaven itself? Here again, however, the important thing is to look, not at what is plausible and insightful today in the spirit of the age, but, rather, at what God wants to tell us, perhaps even through a shift of emphasis.

The doctrine of universal salvation, the conviction that as a matter of principle all men are saved, is widespread today. Even though the sayings about hell, which unmistakably appear in Sacred Scripture and in tradition, are not set aside entirely, many people still have the impression that the fact that there is an eternal punishment simply cannot be God's last word. I admit that I have that feeling, too. And yet we must say: Revelation tells us that this possibility exists.

I am coming here to the decisive point, to the watershed, so to speak, between the faith and the suppositions of the spirit of our age. What precisely does the message of faith tell us now? Jesus says to Nicodemus: "God sent the Son into the world, not to condemn the world, but that the world might be saved through him" (Jn 3:17). That is the core of the Good News. "That the world might be saved" means, nevertheless, that it needs salvation. Perhaps that is the core of the Good News: There is a Savior! but also: We need a Savior! Without him, we are hopelessly lost, each one of us and the whole world. Revelation tells us this. Perdition, eternal unhappiness, is precisely what awaits me if I am not saved. Heaven is not the natural result that can be taken for granted. I must be saved in order to go to heaven. Christ is the Savior and Redeemer. Without him, I sink hopelessly in my lost state. Paul says this quite clearly, echoing the words of the Lord: "God our Savior . . . desires all men to be saved and to come to the knowledge of the truth" (1 Tim 2:4). But if he wants all of us to be saved, then that does mean that all of us are not yet saved. By ourselves we are not saved. God wants to save us, and for that purpose he wants to lead us to the knowledge of the truth.

Is it not exaggerated to say that we are all irremediably lost? On the other hand: Do we have so little personal experience, so little insight into the abyss of our own existence, that we can simply have a false sense of security? Have we never sensed what it means to say: Without you, I am irremediably left to my own devices, trapped in the pit of my own endangerment? The Good News is that God wants all men to be saved. Now perhaps, after all, we understand somewhat better this frightening saying that was quoted at the beginning, the final saying from the Gospel of Mark: "He who believes and is baptized will be saved; but he who does not believe will be condemned" (Mk 16:16). Whoever does not believe that Jesus is his Savior, whoever does not take Jesus' hand, sinks into the abyss of his own perdition. It is not that God will damn him; rather, he himself will sink.

Only One is the Savior, "there is salvation in no one else" (Acts 4:12).

Does hell exist, then? Faith tells us that there is such a thing as saying No to this saving hand of God. That is why we ask that all might come to believe and let themselves be saved by Jesus—or, in other words, that all might convert, either explicitly, by encountering Jesus, or by choosing the good in their lives and following their conscience and thus being saved. But if that is the case, then faith in Jesus Christ is already eternal life now. If I already grasp his hand, then I am in eternal life, even though I must still die. That is why Paul says: "For to me to live is Christ, and to die is gain" (Phil 1:21).

Suggestions for Further Reading

I

Bennett, Rob. *Four Witnesses: The Early Church in Her Own Words: Clement of Rome, Ignatius of Antioch, Justin Martyr, Irenaeus of Lyons.* San Francisco: Ignatius Press, 2002.

Greshake, G. *An den drei-einen Gott glauben: Ein Schlüssel zum Verstehen.* 3rd ed. Freiburg, Basel, and Vienna: Herder, 2000.

Neusner, J. *A Rabbi Talks with Jesus: An Intermillennial, Interfaith Exchange.* New York: Doubleday, 1993.

Stubenrauch, B. *Dreifaltigkeit.* Topos TB 434. Regensburg: Pustet, 2002.

III

Brantschen, J. B. *Warum läßt der gute Gott uns leiden?* New ed. Freiburg, Basel, and Vienna: Herder, 1999.

Julian of Norwich. *The Revelations of Divine Love.* Translated by James Walsh, S.J. New York: Harper, 1961.

IV

International Theological Commission. *Christianity and the World Religions.* September 30, 1996. Vatican City: Libreria Editrice Vaticana, 1997.

Menke, K.-H. *Die Einzigkeit Jesu Christi im Horizont der Sinnfrage.* Kriterien 94. Einsiedeln: Johannes, 1995.

Schimmel, Annemarie. *And Muhammad Is His Messenger: The Veneration of the Prophet in Islamic Piety*. Chapel Hill: University of North Carolina Press, 1985.

V

Kleine Konfessionskunde. Edited by J. A. Möhler-Institut. 2nd ed. Paderborn: Bonifatius, 1997.

Lüning, P. *Ökumene an der Schwelle zum dritten Jahrtausend*. Topos TB 357. Regensburg: Pustet, 2000.

Schönborn, C. *Einheit im Glauben*. Einsiedeln: Johannes, 1984.

VI

Carrell, Alexis. *Man: The Unknown*. New York: Halcyon House, 1938.

Lewis, C. S. *Miracles*. New York: HarperOne, 2009.

VII

Lohfink, G. *Gottes Volksbegehren: Biblische Herausforderungen*. Munich: Neue Stadt, 1998.

Staikos, Metropolit M. *Auferstehung: Von erlebter orthodoxer Spiritualität*. Vienna: Ibera, 2000.

VIII

Beinert, W. *Maria: Spiegel der Erwartungen Gottes und der Menschen*. Topos TB 407. Regensburg: Pustet, 2001.

Ratzinger, J. *Daughter Zion: Meditations on the Church's Marian Belief*. Translated by John M. McDermott. San Francisco: Ignatius Press, 1983.

IX

Augustine. *Confessions*. Translated by Vernon J. Bourke. New York: Fathers of the Church, 1953.

Kehl, M. *Und was kommt nach dem Ende?* 3rd ed. Freiburg, Basel, and Vienna: Herder, 1999.

Schönborn, C. *From Death to Life: The Christian Journey*. Translated by Brian McNeil. San Francisco: Ignatius Press, 1995.